D0188886

Sacramental Magic

in a Small-Town Café

ALSO BY BROTHER PETER REINHART

Brother Juniper's Bread Book

SACRAMENTAL MAGIC
in a
Small-Town Café

Recipes and Stories from

Brother Juniper's Café

BR. PETER REINHART

ADDISON-WESLEY PUBLISHING COMPANY

Reading, Massachusetts   Menlo Park, California   New York
Don Mills, Ontario   Wokingham, England   Amsterdam   Bonn
Sydney   Singapore   Tokyo   Madrid   San Juan
Paris   Seoul   Milan   Mexico City   Taipei

Many of the designations used by manufacturers and sellers to distinguish their products are claimed as trademarks. Where those designations appear in this book and Addison-Wesley was aware of a trademark claim, the designations have been printed in initial capital letters (e.g., PacMan).

The ideas and thoughts contained in this book are solely those of the author, and in no way should be considered official doctrine or policy of Christ the Saviour Brotherhood or any other organization.

Library of Congress Cataloging-in-Publication Data

Reinhart, Peter.
    Sacramental magic in a small-town cafe : recipes and stories from Brother Juniper's Cafe / Peter Reinhart.
        p.   cm.
    Includes index.

    1. Cookery.   2. Brother Juniper's Cafe.   I. Title.
TX714.R445   1994
641.5—dc20
                                                94-26448
                                                 CIP

Copyright © 1994 by Brother Peter Reinhart

All rights reserved. No part of this publication may be reproduced, stored in a retrieval system, or transmitted, in any form or by any means, electronic, mechanical, photocopying, recording, or otherwise, without the prior written permission of the publisher. Printed in the United States of America. Published simultaneously in Canada.

Jacket design by Jean Seal
Jacket art by Michèle Manning
Text design by Linda Koegel
Set in 10.5-point Sabon by Weimer

To Ted Reinhart and Russ Thayer,
whose lives were a testament of integrity
and who continue supporting me
from a higher vantage point

"*Mercy and truth, my friends, have met together,*" *said the General.*
"*Righteousness and bliss shall kiss one another. . . . Man, my friends . . .*
is frail and foolish. We have all of us been told that grace is to be found
in the universe. But in our human foolishness and short-sightedness we
imagine divine grace to be finite. For this reason we tremble . . ." *Never*
till now had the General stated that he trembled; he was genuinely
surprised and even shocked at hearing his own voice proclaim the fact.
"*We tremble before making our choice in life, and after having made it*
again tremble in fear of having chosen wrong. But the moment comes
when our eyes are opened, and we see and realize that grace is infinite.
Grace, brothers, makes no conditions and singles out none of us in
particular; grace takes us all to its bosom and proclaims general amnesty.
See! that which we have chosen is given us, and that which we have
refused is, also and at the same time, granted us. Ay, that which we have
rejected is poured upon us abundantly. For mercy and truth have met
together, and righteousness and bliss have kissed one another!"

General Loewenheim in *Babette's Feast*
by Isak Dinesen

My dear people,
let us love one another
since love comes from God
and every one who loves is begotten by God and knows God.
Anyone who fails to love can never have known God,
because God is love.

I John 4:7–8
Jerusalem Bible

Love and business and family and religion and art and patriotism are
nothing but shadows of words when a man is starving.

O. Henry

Contents

୧ GUMBO, CHILI, & SOUPS

BARBECUE

❧ TONICS

❧ BREADS, MUFFINS, & SCONES

🐦 A FEW DESSERTS

Acknowledgments

૨ം First and foremost, I owe an unpayable debt of gratitude to my wife Susan, who developed many of the recipes in this book and who continues to feed me in ways that make restaurants seem superfluous. The warm feeling evoked by Brother Juniper's Café was a direct result of her special touches, sensitivities, and vision.

Elizabeth Carduff, my editor at Addison-Wesley, has been a joy. She kept me on track and provided encouragement and direction whenever I needed it. And I think we like food in the same way.

The rest of the Addison-Wesley support team (and I truly understand, better than ever, the collaborative nature of putting out a book) has been wonderful. Special thanks to Beth Burleigh, Jean Seal, Pat Jalbert, Evie Righter, and Linda Koegel. They took a raw casserole of a book and baked it into a beautiful finished dish. Also, thanks to Len Gilbert for his marketing support during the past few years.

Thanks also to my unofficial press agent, Phoebe Leider (aka Phyllis Reinhart), whom I have known for forty-four years as Mom. I think she has sold more books and generated more publicity than the rest of us put together.

A whole community of people made Brother Juniper's Café a "local legend." In addition to the people of Forestville, and the wider circle of Sonoma County (which I only semi-laughingly call the "culinary center of the universe"), there are our brothers and sisters from Christ the Saviour Brotherhood, many of whom helped in ways seen and unseen. There are also the kids from El Molino High School who apprenticed with us at the café, and the many other employees who shared in the work, most notably Rob Stickley, who ended an around-the-world bicycle tour with a stint as our lead cook. I would especially like to thank Mara Jennings, who has outlasted us all and continues to be the heart and soul of Brother Juniper's Bakery. Thanks also to Tim Decker, Sal Ceja, Juan Soto, Mike Woods, and Terry Good, who have kept the wheels turning during the last few years. The cast and crew is an ever changing organism, so I thank you all, past and present, for making Brother Juniper's a place worth writing about.

Finally, an important thanks to Ron and Lorene Colvin, the proud (and exhausted) new owners of Brother Juniper's Bakery. They have begun the arduous task of taking Brother Juniper's to the next level, fulfilling its potential as a socially responsible and philanthropic business. I wish them God's blessings on the mission ahead, knowing full well how much work it takes to realize such a vision. They are special people.

Preface

❧ "Remember, Peter, you are writing a food book, not a philosophy book." This advice, given a number of times by my various editors, has guided me through both *Brother Juniper's Bread Book* and now this, *Sacramental Magic in a Small-Town Café*. M. F. K. Fisher, just before her passing, reminded me never to talk down to readers. "Don't preach—tell them a story." Her wisdom has been a lamp unto my feet.

When we started Brother Juniper's Café in 1986 it was conceived as an extension of our ministry as members of a Christian Order. We quickly realized that the ministry aspect would never bear fruit if the food was not wonderful. My wife Susan and I believe in feeding body as well as soul. If we did not, this book and the stories in it would never have come to pass.

There is still, despite the warnings, quite a bit of philosophy and religion in this book. I learned after *Brother Juniper's Bread Book* that there was a greater hunger and appreciation for it than anyone expected. I hope you will forgive me for indulging in the troublesome habit (to the editors, anyway) of extending my metaphors. I have, admirably I think, restrained myself, but the extensions excite me, like a good punchline. I want you to have the thrill of drawing your own conclusions, having your own flashes, but I cannot resist sharing some of my own. I hope that you will feel that I struck a fair balance.

There is a relatively new product on the market: It is called Beano and is an enzyme that is supposed to help us digest beans without the usual fanfare. One drop, it says on the bottle, is all it takes.

Enzyme action—I like that. It is like leavening, where a few grains of yeast can raise an entire loaf. I pretty much exhausted that metaphor in the last book, and Beano is not so pretty, or as cosmic. However, here's hoping that the pages to follow will perform like that potent drop of enzyme, and function as a catalytic converter leading to your own insights, your very own flash.

The Vision:

An Introduction

꿈 Brother Juniper's Café began as a vision, crashed to earth, broke our backs, threatened our well-being, almost went bankrupt, rose from the ashes (carrying us with it), spawned a bakery and then a book, restored our hope, and, after seven years, appears to have landed on its feet, having somehow manifested its unspoken mission—sacramental magic. Looking back, the café had been fulfilling this mission all along but we were too fatigued to notice. It is called the cost of doing business.

What is this sacramental magic, this vision, and how could such a noble sounding goal cause so much pain along its sacred way? I am going to attempt to tell you the story, punctuating it with wonderful recipes that will provide only some of the ingredients of this delicious and elusive moment that I have too glibly called "sacramental magic." The sheer ambition of the title should give a sense of the enormity of the weight that we, my wife Susan and I, shouldered in attempting something far beyond our skills and stamina. That we endured to tell the story gives us some satisfaction; that there is a story to tell is providential; that you are at all interested in hearing the story is sheer grace.

This is a book about the things I learned during the past seven years, about the importance of food not as nourishment alone.

Many writers have written of their passion for food and a few special ones have opened with their words an appetite for understanding. There are infinite ways to reach the subtle realms but none are so enjoyable, yet potent, as those that begin with food.

After many years of praying, studying, and yes, eating, I have come up with a theory. Brother Juniper's Café did not originate because of this theory, but it did unfold it to me. It boils down to this: Every meal we eat has a hidden unrealized potential to re-create the mystery of the Last Supper, the Paschal Feast, the entry of the Uncreated into creation. God, the Creative Force, Shakti, Bodhi, whatever you call it (I call it God), infuses all and uses all as a bridge. The problem is we rarely, if ever, realize it. Religions and spiritual practices have taught this simple fact for centuries but most of us have had only fleeting, teasing glimpses of it. The rare vision, if it occurs at all, often appears around food, during a meal, at a special time in a special place. To have had even one taste of such a moment confirms the spiritual intuition that each of us carries into the world. Every meal, whether we are conscious of it or not, is a form of communion.

Religions teach methods to sensitize ourselves to this reality, but most people have abandoned spiritual practice. Of those who do practice, few can articulate why, nor would they put it in the context I have chosen. That is because they have never worked at Brother Juniper's Café.

My thesis is this: that each of us unknowingly yearns for a communion experience every time we eat. Years of neglect have numbed us to this desire, this spiritual passion, but a still, small part of ourselves never forgets, it merely lays patiently waiting. Sometimes, as if by chance, or grace, a connection is made. It is in those moments that sacramental magic occurs.

Food is not only a basic human need, it is also a sacred symbol: God in a multitude of forms and bodies. It is a focal point of fellowship and celebration. The cooking of food is also an artistic practice. Its potency ranges from physical necessity to grand metaphoric and allegorical dimensions. Food both nourishes and kills us, and is simultaneously icon and idol. Restaurants are like secular churches, home of both *eros* and *agape,* in which the latent possibility of sacramental magic always exists.

Brother Juniper's Café existed as such a restaurant for a brief three years and touched the hearts and souls of its patrons in subtle, unexpected ways. When it closed, changing formats to a bakery café to accommodate the growth of Brother Juniper's Bakery, the neighborhood response was a mixture of understanding and upset. Some townspeople formed a volunteer committee to try to keep it open. Others felt betrayed, as if their access to hope (also affordable good food) had been denied. Five years later we still receive requests to reopen the restaurant, and there is great disappointment when we express our unwillingness to comply.

Food can touch people on many levels. This is the story of a café that affected people as if it were a church, of the food it served, and why it evoked such passion.

For those who have read *Brother Juniper's Bread Book: Slow Rise as Method and Metaphor,* this new book will be a prequel historically, but a sequel thematically. This effort explores more deeply the connection between food and spirit, eating and worship, and the multi-dimensionality of God. As the word *sacrament* derives from root words meaning "mystery" and "sacred feast," this book is about how we all mysteriously yearn for a sacred feast every time we eat. It is also the story of our culinary pilgrimage as it manifested through the phenomenon known as Brother Juniper's Café. It tells about what we learned and what can occur when magic is present. This is really a story about the possibility of magic, which is, after all, what people want more than anything else.

Prologue:

Brother Juniper's Café and the

Elements of Magic

🙟 We are not Franciscans but ever since 1968 our Order, Christ the Saviour Brotherhood (formerly known as the Holy Order of MANS), has operated restaurants all over the world dedicated to the spirit of a famous Franciscan monk named Brother Juniper. Though each restaurant is different, they are places where all are welcome, the coffee is good, and charitable works occur.

The original Brother Juniper is chronicled in the legends of St. Francis of Assisi. He was St. Francis's favorite monk because he was simple, humble, and generous. He came home naked on occasion because beggars asked him for alms and all he had was the cassock on his back. According to a story in *The Little Flowers of St. Francis,* he was not a particularly good cook, having once tried to boil a chicken with all its feathers. He was somewhat of a simpleton, known in the Christian tradition as a Fool for Christ. Few appreciate these kinds of people until after they die. While alive they make everyone around them nervous because they are so unpredictable, so unbeholden to convention and worldliness. Every community needs them but does not really want them in its midst. The eight-hundred-year lineage of Franciscans named Juniper, including Father Junipero Serra, the famous peripatetic priest who established the Franciscan missions throughout California, have all descended from the original twelfth-century monk named Brother Juniper.

When we opened our café in 1986, we chose to walk in the tradition of the Brother Juniper's restaurants already in existence, but our menu took on a completely different character; we had some new ideas.

Brother Juniper's Café

Susan and I were staff members at our Order's retreat center in Forestville, a small town about seventy miles north of San Francisco, in the wine country of Sonoma County. We lived in a semimonastic community, which means that there were both single and married members, all living a life under religious vows. Sister Susan, as she was known, and I were engaged to be married. She was the cook for the retreat center community, which consisted of about twenty-five permanent residents and a never-ending stream of guests on spiritual retreats or in for seminars.

Among my tasks were the making of beeswax candles for use in our chapels around the country, tending the hives, helping with the organic garden, working editorially for *Epiphany Journal* (a quarterly theological magazine), and, unofficially, kibbitzing with Susan in the kitchen whenever possible.

I was also working on the development of potential food products around which to build a community business. This included making cheese twice a week in our driveway in a makeshift cheese tank, aging the rolled curds (called wheels) in the community walk-in refrigerator, which eventually gave all the shelves and food a bluish moldlike tint. I told everyone I was developing my own penicillin, but they never bought the story.

To get myself through the hot summer days, I made large batches of various syrups with fresh ginger, herbs, lemons, limes, honey, and miscellaneous tree barks. Then I would mix the syrups with water and ice and drink about two quarts a day. Those syrups eventually evolved into ginger fizz and other sodas. My most passionate food experiment was making barbecue sauce, of which I have more to tell in a later chapter.

Bread always played a central role in the seasonal and spiritual festivals that we celebrated. A few of us were avid bread bakers, so we often took turns trying out new ideas or attempting to render ancient and forgotten bread formulas that we dug out of old books. Struan bread, which is featured in my first book, was the most remarkable discovery of all this baking. I also learned how to get great crust on French bread, a trick that was to win us friends and several awards.

There were many talented cooks and musicians in our community, which meant there was a constant sense of festivity. Certain brothers or sisters, known for skill at cooking particular ethnic foods, got the call when a Mexican, Italian, or other cultural festival was at hand. Birthdays were an excuse to try out new recipes or to present an old family favorite. These celebrations usually included an original skit or play, often built around an idiosyncratic aspect of the birthday celebrant. This provided an entertaining and humorous way to acknowledge our appreciation for each other; we became skilled skit writers.

We celebrated all of this festivity in the context of a larger vision, to bring traditional methods for the transmission of knowledge into contemporary life. Viewing life as a series of initiations, the motivating question was, "How is wisdom passed from one generation to the next, and how can a modern society support and value the knowledge of elders?" This quest for what we called an "initiatic life" provided us with a sense of mission in all of our work and play. We sought ways to apply our findings through service to the poor, curriculum development for primary schools, spiritual practice (prayer, fasting, and participation in the sacramental and liturgical life), the recovery of traditional celebrations and festivals, and a search to create appropriate livelihood through craftsmanship.

My personal goal was to set up a food business that would eventually provide enough jobs and income to support a whole community. We had so many talented cooks that it seemed a logical direction. The idea was to establish a small restaurant to showcase our various products, eventually spinning some of them off as separate operations such as bakeries, packaging companies for soups, sauces, and dressings, and a beverage business.

After months of searching for a place, we found a small cookie store in downtown Forestville that was preparing to close ("downtown" is a somewhat hyperbolic description in a town that boasts a constant population of 1,776 people). It cost about $25,000 to renovate the little shop, bringing the kitchen up to code, remodeling, collecting the equipment, utensils, and serving dishes, then getting all the necessary licenses and permits. All of this became a crash course on working in the world after ten years "behind the monastery walls." Before long I was well acquainted with both the concept and reality of stress.

Susan and I headed up the project for the community while we also prepared ourselves for marriage, following a two-year courtship. We divided the responsibilities. Susan was in charge of decor and ambiance, and for developing the pastries, salads, soups, and specials. I was in charge of the chili and gumbo, barbecue, bread, and natural sodas, as well as the bookkeeping and public relations. Some of the mechanically skilled members of our community helped with the renovation. After three months of preparation we opened on April Fool's Day of 1986, an irony that we came to appreciate more fully in the years to follow. And a few months after we opened Brother Juniper's Café, Susan and I were married.

The Elements of Magic

Susan always stressed that it was the little things that mattered and she became the master of the small touches that laid a foundation for what I now call the *possibility of magic*.

She created a closet full of seasonal and holiday material, including decorations, poems, artwork, and historical information. This enabled her to instantly change the feel of the place, keeping it in tune with the natural cycles and some of the more special festivals like Michaelmas (September 29), Christmas, Easter, and even St. Valentine's Day.

One of Susan's touches was a children's area that had a small rocking chair, a collection of storybooks and dolls, and framed lithographs from old fairy and folktales. This area kept small children happily entertained, enabling their parents to linger over their meals a few extra minutes, and provided the kids with a sense of place whenever they returned. Many of the children who became regulars treated this area in much the same way an adult treats the newspaper and magazine section of a favorite coffee house, checking out the rack to see if there were any new arrivals.

Another touch that became part of the unique personality of Brother Juniper's Café was the peanut men, who came out every year like little elves to inhabit the Christmas tree. The peanut men were made by one of the brothers, Br. Gary, who remembered them from his childhood. He took unshelled peanuts, pushed pipe cleaners through the shells to make arms and legs, created faces with marking pens and typewriter correction fluid, and dipped the tops in melted crayons to make hats. Every peanut took on a personality of its own and they made great ornaments for the tree, hanging like acrobats from the branches and balls. There were always plenty of extra peanut men to give to the kids for their own trees at home.

Our lives were enriched, and so was the business, by the hiring of developmentally disabled adults. Some were with us for many years, providing an aspect of kindness and gentleness to the company that seems to bring out the best in the other employees.

Establishing a business in a small town also gave us the opportunity to employ local high school students and be a part of their growing up. In addition to their work, they became a bridge that enabled us to integrate ourselves with the greater community, no easy task after living in seclusion. Some parents encouraged their kids to seek jobs with us because they felt we would be a good influence on them. As a result, we became friends with both the students and their parents.

While the business was growing and we were learning our lessons, the brotherhood community was going through some major revisions. The Order changed from a nondenominational, independent Order, and joined the Eastern Orthodox Church under a Greek Orthodox bishop. Many of the married couples and families were moving toward independent living and economic self-sufficiency. The communal model that had worked so well for us for our first twenty years now seemed more appropriate only for those who had committed themselves to a traditional monastic life, about 10 percent of our community.

The retreat center was rededicated as a monastery, under the guidance of Abbot Herman, a Russian monk who had joined our Order and brought all of the monks and nuns from his two monasteries with him. There are now small monastic enclaves throughout the country, functioning cooperatively with the householder segment of the community.

Many of us now live in our own homes and own businesses. Susan and I bought Brother Juniper's from the Order in 1990 as we realized that the community-based business we had earlier envisioned would no longer work, as many of our members moved to other parts of the country.

Despite the changes around us, one thing that never changed, superseding any business and livelihood objectives of Brother Juniper's, was its ministerial purpose: to help those in need and to touch the hearts and souls of all who came through the door. This was epitomized by the Poor People's Cup.

One day, a few months after we opened, Father (Abbot) Herman came in for lunch. He was a frequent visitor to the café and would often have meetings with some of his monks at a corner table. We usually tried to treat him to a meal but he always insisted on paying. However, on this day, he gave us five dollars extra and suggested we start a poor people's cup to buy a meal for someone who could not afford to pay. "After all," he said, "I may not be able to pay some day and it would be nice to know that the charity of others might feed me."

We pulled out a paper cup, one of those large soup-to-go cups, and wrote across the front, Poor People's Cup. That is all we did or said. We put that cup on the counter and within months there was so much money in it that we not only bought meals for the few travelers who stumbled in asking for help, but used it to buy substantial groceries for several poor families in the area. Every Christmas and Easter we depleted the cup by adopting one or more families and buying groceries and presents for the kids. It never took long for the cup to replenish itself.

The ease with which our customers donated to the cup amazed me. Later we added a fishbowl earmarked specifically for Raphael House, the homeless shelter our Order runs in San Francisco. Gratefully, we watched both the cup and the bowl continually fill. During the past seven years we have sent thousands of dollars to Raphael House, and fed and clothed dozens of others, because of the charitable contributions made by our customers.

Susan and I were both quite sobered by the discretionary responsibility entrusted to us. Rarely did anyone ever question where or how the money was spent. There was enough coming through the cup to make it available to others who knew of needy people and they would call us. I came to believe that many who donated did so because of a desire to actively participate in the Brother Juniper's ministry. It was an acknowledgment of their connectedness to what we were trying to accomplish, a living symbol of their support and approval.

This was the context in which Brother Juniper's Café, for three short yet long years, existed. It became the crucible, or as the spiritual elders call it, *the arena,* in which we discovered our mission and worked out our destiny, abandoning ourselves, as the saying goes, to divine providence. What follows are some of the things we did and learned along the way.

MARINADES

&

CONDIMENTS

Symbiosis:

The Gravity of Condiments

❧ I first learned about symbiotic and synergistic relationships in a classic science fiction novel by Olaf Stapledon called *Starmaker*. In it he describes other planets and galaxies in which survival and the evolution of consciousness depend on instinctual and learned cooperation between species. The best symbiotic relationships, according to Stapledon, lead to an action called synergy, which, explained loosely, means that the sum is greater than its parts (in classical theology the term *synergy* refers to the efforts of humans meeting the unearned grace of God, leading to the experience of salvation).

Most of us know the fable of the scorpion and the frog, in which the punch line is that the scorpion, giving in to its inherent nature, stings the frog even after the frog has transported it across a river. In Stapledon's worlds the scorpion would come to control its proclivity, and the frog and scorpion would then learn to work together for the betterment of the planet.

I am using a rather obtuse way of getting around to the subject, but often I find myself thinking about *Starmaker* when I open my refrigerator. It is almost completely filled with condiments. It has been like this since 1986, when Susan and I, having just opened Brother Juniper's Café, got married. We are both inveterate condiment freaks. A number of years earlier, when Susan celebrated her birthday while working as a pastor's assistant at a Lutheran church in San Francisco, her co-workers gave her twenty bottles of hot pepper sauce, saying it was the only thing they were sure she would absolutely use. I, likewise, long before developing Holy Smoke Barbecue Sauce, had assembled a collection of barbecue sauces from all over the country, which I would bring out at various gatherings for blind tastings and judging. Our refrigerator is full of salsas, seasoning pastes, concentrates, garlic dips, mustards, salad dressings, and just about anything else we come across that looks intriguing when we go out shopping. The payoff for this extremism is that we get to keep telling ourselves, "Gee, we can make this (and make it better!)." We have also learned to follow this up with, "But why bother."

There is one good reason to bother and that is because salsas, dips, and sauces are easy to make and fun to eat. While we sometimes discover some exceptional, hard-to-top products in the stores, the ones made at home, following proper food sense and a passionate palate, are often better. For instance, I have never figured out why there are so many mediocre salsas on the market when it is quite simple to make exceptional salsa. It is interesting that salsa now outsells catsup, considering how difficult it is to make good catsup and how easy it is to make good salsa.

Most of our homemade condiments developed as a consequence of a shared love for spicy food. Many of the things we make, such as the recipes to follow, are simply variations built around a potent hot peppermash made from a blend of chiles and garlic. The mash acts as a base from which many exciting combinations are possible. Some enterprising folks in San Luis Obispo, for example, have been putting out a mail-order catalogue for a few years called "Mo Hotta-Mo Betta." They feature over a hundred condiments, including Brother Juniper's Holy

Smoke Barbecue Sauce, that have "heat" as the common thread. Surprisingly, our hottest sauce is categorized only as medium in their catalogue, which says quite a bit about the gustatory tolerance of a growing segment of society.

Condiments are gravity centers. They carry a disproportionate amount of flavor that gives them weightiness. Condiments are concentrated, with an intensity that seems always to be on the verge of exploding, and it does, on the palate, when a condiment is used properly. The trick is to take advantage of this explosiveness, which brings me back to symbiosis and synergy.

An example of culinary symbiosis, or the complementarity of foods, is French fries with catsup, or malt vinegar. Other examples are chips and salsa, curry and chutney, or ribs and barbecue sauce. One of my favorite examples of symbiosis is barbecue and coleslaw, about which I've written extensively and passionately. The result of good barbecue sauce intermingling on the plate and the palate with properly prepared coleslaw is a perfect illustration of symbiosis leading to synergy.

The following condiment, marinade, and sauce recipes illustrate more nobly than words the principles of symbiosis and synergy. For a still deeper understanding, I refer you to *Starmaker*.

ે Ginger Curry Marinade

MAKES 1 1/2 CUPS

We use this to marinate tofu (see barbecued tofu, page 144) but it is also excellent for lamb, especially lamb shish kebabs, and other meats. When marinating tofu be sure to use only extra-firm tofu and drain off all excess water. The marinade will keep for weeks in the refrigerator. It can be reused after one batch of tofu but will begin to thin because of the water in the curd. After marinating a second batch of tofu it would be best to discard the remaining marinade. After marinating meat, you can get another round from the marinade by bringing what remains to a boil and simmering it for one minute, which will kill any bacteria from the meat.

1 cup olive oil
¼ cup fresh lemon juice, strained
2 tablespoons minced or grated onion
1 tablespoon peeled and minced ginger
1 tablespoon curry powder
2 large cloves garlic, coarsely chopped
½ tablespoon crushed dried chile peppers
½ tablespoon whole coriander seeds
1 tablespoon salt

In a large bowl mix together all the ingredients. Marinate meats and tofu, covered, for a minimum of 4 hours or overnight in the refrigerator.

❧ Brother Juniper's Chile Peppermash

MAKES ABOUT 10 CUPS

The base for many of our creations, this peppermash is easy to make and will last indefinitely. Once you have a supply of it you will find dozens of uses, such as in the marinades to follow or as a table condiment. My favorite pepper for this is the red jalapeño, which is sweeter than the green and has just the right balance of heat and pulp. Serrano peppers are slightly hotter but smaller, which means more work to stem them. They do not have as much pulp either. However, the best mash of all is made by blending a variety of peppers: Anaheim and Fresno peppers have the pulp but little heat, so they are good for mild mashes. Habanero or Scotch bonnet peppers are the hottest, so be extremely careful; each is seventy times hotter than a jalapeño.

Use only fresh, not dried, peppers for this mash.

3 pounds fresh red chiles, preferably red jalapeño peppers, if
   available
4½ cups red wine vinegar
10 large cloves garlic, peeled
3 tablespoons salt

Wash and stem the peppers. In a blender or food processor, purée all the ingredients until smooth. (You will need to process the mixture in batches. Do not pack the peppers too tightly or you may overload your blender or food processor.)

Step back from the blender when removing the lid as pepper gas may be released and it will sting your eyes. Also, be careful when tasting this mash as it may be very spicy.

Store the mash in a plastic container, not in a canning jar (it will react to the metal lid, corroding it). Refrigerated, this mash keeps indefinitely.

Susan's Salsas

The two salsas that follow are easy to make and outperform any salsas I have ever purchased. Many of our customers would sim-

ply order a roll, or two slices of bread, and then help themselves to the complimentary salsa. I have to admit, it made a pretty good meal.

🐦 Spicy Red Salsa

HOT!—MAKES 4 CUPS

One 28-ounce can diced tomatoes with juice (During tomato season you can substitute 2 pounds fresh tomatoes, but this fresh salsa must be eaten within a day or two.)
4 large cloves garlic, finely minced
2 fresh green jalapeño peppers, stemmed and finely diced (Use 1 for a milder salsa.)
½ medium onion, diced
¼ cup coarsely chopped fresh cilantro
¾ teaspoon salt
2 tablespoons cider vinegar
¼ teaspoon dried oregano

Mix all the ingredients together, including the juice from the tomatoes. If using fresh tomatoes, you will need to increase the salt, to taste.

Refrigerate in a plastic container with a good lid. The salsa will keep for 4 days—it begins to ferment after that but it will probably be consumed by then!

❧ Green Salsa

MAKES 5 CUPS

One 28-ounce can tomatillos (Mexican green tomatoes), with
  juice*
1 small onion, quartered
7 fresh serrano or 5 fresh jalapeño peppers, stemmed
½ cup coarsely chopped fresh cilantro
1 avocado, seeded and scooped (optional)
3 large cloves garlic
Salt, to taste

Purée all the ingredients, including the tomatillo juice, in a
blender or food processor. Tomatillos tend to gelatinize after
about 24 hours. If they do, add ¼ cup water to the salsa and stir.
The avocado will also prevent gelatinizing. If using fresh tomatillos, which are available in some parts of the country, you will
need to add more salt and ¼ cup white vinegar.

Store in a tightly sealed plastic container for up to 4
days.

NOTE: For a smoky variation on either the red or green
salsa, substitute *chipotle* chile peppers for the serrano or jalape-
ños. *Chipotles* are smoked jalapeño peppers in a very hot adobo
sauce. They can be found in small cans in many markets in the
Mexican foods section.

*You may substitute an equal amount of fresh tomatillos, approxi-
mately 3½ cups. Remove them from their papery covering and blanch them
for 1 minute in boiling, salted water before puréeing them. See additional
adjustments above.

Marinades/Sauces

This is where a supply of peppermash really pays off because it forms the base of many of our marinade and sauce recipes. We discovered that there are infinite variations on the sweet/sour/hot theme. They are all delicious and can be used not only as marinades but also as stir-fry and pasta sauces. And recently we found a new use for them—as a dipping sauce for corn on the cob.

Two marinades can be made and then be combined for more complexity. For instance, I like to mix apricot marinade with orange cilantro marinade. The variations are almost infinite, limited only by your sense of daring.

An ingredient note: If you do not have any Brother Juniper's Chile Peppermash on hand, there are commercial products that can be substituted. They can be found in the Oriental foods section of many supermarkets or in Asian specialty markets, under the generic name Chile Garlic Sauce.

❧ Apricot or Fruited Sauce/Marinade

MAKES ABOUT 8 CUPS

This recipe makes a thick sauce, especially good as the finish for a stir-fried dish such as Chinese vegetables or on spicy noodles. By adding 1 cup olive oil, the sauce becomes a marinade, in which you can flavor and tenderize meat, seafood, poultry, or tofu.

6 cups pitted coarsely chopped fresh apricots (about 20 small
   apricots)*
½–1 cup Brother Juniper's Chile Peppermash (page 6—use
   according to your chile tolerance)
½ cup fresh lemon juice
1 cup sugar
4 tablespoons peeled and grated or finely minced fresh ginger
1 cup olive oil (for marinade only)

NOTE: A variation of this marinade can be made by adding 1 tablespoon of either curry powder or cumin seed. Because
they will dramatically change the flavor, I suggest not using them
until you have made the basic marinade and used it. Add them at
another time when you want a Southwestern or east Indian
flavor. Try these and other spices to create flavors appropriate for
the meal at hand.

In a large saucepan, combine all ingredients except the olive
oil and reserving half the lemon juice. Bring the mixture to a boil
over medium-high heat. Stir to break up the fruit, simmering for
about 10 minutes until the sugar is dissolved and everything is
thoroughly cooked and soft. Remove the pan from the heat, add
the remaining lemon juice, and let cool.

Press the mixture through a food mill or purée it in a
blender or food processor until smooth, adding the olive oil if it

---

*You may substitute plums, grapes (remove seeds or use seedless
grapes; chop to release the juice), pineapple, and peeled peaches or nectarines. Some fruits go better with certain foods, such as pineapple with ham
and fish, peaches and nectarines with poultry, grapes with lamb, and plums
with roast pork. Experiment, looking for the symbiotic relationships that
work for your palate.

is to be used strictly as a marinade. Store the sauce or marinade in the refrigerator, where it will keep for 1 week, or freeze it.

❧ Caribbean Orange Cilantro Marinade

MAKES 2 1/2 CUPS
This is terrific with shrimp and other seafood.

1 cup orange juice concentrate
1 cup extra-virgin olive oil
5 tablespoons balsamic vinegar
1/4 cup Brother Juniper's Chile Peppermash (page 6)
1/4 cup chopped fresh cilantro
1/4 teaspoon salt
1/8 teaspoon freshly ground black pepper

Combine all the ingredients in a large bowl, mixing well with a wire whisk.

This marinade should be used the day it is made. If it is not, store in a plastic container in the freezer, where it will keep for up to 6 months.

❧ Fajitas Marinade

ENOUGH FOR 6
Fajitas, or Mexican stir-fried platters, are growing in popularity nationwide. They are fun and easy to serve at home, especially

*with this marinade for meat, chicken, or vegetables. In case you
have never made or seen fajitas, I am including Susan's version,
which makes a great family dinner.*

½ cup soy sauce
½ cup Worcestershire sauce (Lea & Perrins is preferred)
½ cup fresh lemon juice
6 tablespoons extra-virgin olive oil
12 large cloves garlic, minced
1 large onion, finely chopped
2 medium green bell peppers, seeded and diced
2 tomatoes, finely chopped
½ cup chopped fresh cilantro
2 teaspoons salt
2 teaspoons freshly ground black pepper

Whisk all the ingredients together in a large bowl. You may
marinate up to 3 pounds meat, poultry, or assorted vegetables in
this mixture. Here is an example of how to use it:

ଌ Susan's Steak Fajitas

SERVES 6 *

*You may substitute boned chicken or vegetables, but not leafy ones.
Some vegetables that work well in this dish are zucchini, yellow summer
squash, red and green bell peppers, broccoli and cauliflower florets, mushrooms, onions, and fresh green beans. Slice the vegetables ¼ inch thick and
allow about ½ pound assorted vegetables per person.

~ GENERAL NOTES ABOUT MARINATING

• When marinating beef, chicken, or pork, coat the meat thoroughly with the marinade, chill for 2 or more hours, then cook it as desired (grilled, baked, sautéed, and so on). Seafood should only marinate up to 1½ hours; after that the acids in the marinade begin to break down the protein in the seafood.

• If using a marinade as a sauce or gravy, heat it in a saucepan and serve it at the table in a gravy boat or pour it over the food as it cooks. For marinades used with meat, poultry, or seafood, be sure to bring them to a boil to kill any bac-

3 pounds skirt steak
¼ pound mushrooms, sliced
1 large onion, sliced into half-moon strips
1 teaspoon olive oil

Cut the steak across the grain into strips ½ inch wide and 2 inches long. The slices should be sliced as uniformly as possible, for even cooking, and no thicker than ⅛ inch. It may be easier to do this with partially frozen meat.

Place the meat in a bowl and pour the marinade over it. Toss so that it covers the meat evenly. Cover and marinate for 1 hour in the refrigerator.

Add the mushrooms and onions. Mix well, cover, and refrigerate 1 hour more.

teria that may have been transmitted from the meat or seafood.

· In stir-fries, add the marinade-sauce (the one made without oil) at the last moment and stir until hot.

· In pasta dishes, toss the heated marinade-sauce with the noodles until coated.

· If glazing meat or poultry, brush the marinade-sauce on during the final 15 minutes of roasting.

· Lastly, you can serve many marinades as a simple condiment, like a chutney or dipping sauce, at the table. The fruited marinades, made without oil, are especially appropriate used this way.

Pour the meat, mushrooms, and onions through a sieve or colander into a bowl, reserving all excess marinade. Put the marinade in a saucepan and bring it to a boil. Keep it hot until serving time.

Over a high flame or setting, heat a fajitas pan (flat, oblong skillet), or a cast-iron frying pan until very hot. Add the olive oil and spread to coat the pan (if your pan is small, divide the mixture and use 2 pans). Add the meat/vegetable mixture and stir-fry for about 3 minutes, or until all the meat is cooked and tender. Remove from the heat.

Set a hot pad or trivet on the table and place the fajitas pan on it. The meat is customarily wrapped in warm flour tortillas and served with any of the following: rice, refried beans, salsa fresca (chopped tomato, green chiles, onion, cilantro, lemon juice, salt, and pepper), green or red salsa, sour cream, grated Cheddar cheese, guacamole or sliced avocado. Serve the hot marinade in a pitcher on the side. If you want to spice the meal up, serve the fajitas with the following *Chipotles* Cream.

ໃ⬤ *Chipotles* Cream

MAKES ABOUT 1 ¹/₄ CUPS

1 cup sour cream
2 (canned) *chipotles* peppers, finely chopped
2 tablespoons adobo sauce (the sauce in which the *chipotles* are packed in the can)

Mix well. This will keep, covered, in the refrigerator for up to 1 week.

SALADS

&

PICKLES

There Is No Greek Salad on

Mount Athos

❧ When our nondenominational, independent Order decided to enter the Eastern Orthodox Church in 1987, the decision brought with it extensive culture shock. One of the main challenges was a reorientation from a Roman Catholic clerical garb (our Order was originally modeled on the Jesuits) to either a monastic cassock or civilian clothing. For many of us, getting used to civvies, and not having a collar to identify us as religious ministers, caused a deep re-visioning of ourselves and our mission. A number of our members saw this as an opportunity to make pilgrimages to well-known holy shrines. Susan and I, for instance, went to the British Isles and visited the famous Celtic monasteries at Iona, Lindisfarne, and many churches throughout Ireland. Some of our members went to Jerusalem to retrace the steps of Jesus through the Via Dolorosa.

A few others made the difficult journey to Mount Athos, the location of twenty monasteries of varying degrees of strictness and pattern, considered the heart of Eastern Orthodox monasticism. No women are allowed to set foot on this northern Greek peninsula, a bastion of male aloneness. The diet is strictly vegetarian and quite bland. Monks are not expected to be too concerned with health or nutritional issues as they follow an ancient set of dietary fasts and rituals. They are not supposed to enjoy food but to eat only what is necessary to keep their bodies alive, freeing them to focus on prayer, meditation, and study. It is a narrow, rigorous path to which few are called.

Mount Athos is the one place in Greece where you will not find Greek salad. I doubt, also, that there is any place in Greece that makes a salad as good as the one we served at Brother Juniper's. I cannot prove the veracity of this bold statement, but I do know that I never experienced a Greek salad as good in any of my travels.

The distinguishing characteristic of Greek salad is the feta cheese used in it. In Greece, feta is a strong cheese, made with milk from either sheep or goats. In this country a milder, less expensive version is made from cow's milk. What is most distinctive about our version of Greek salad is the dressing, which incorporates domestic feta as an ingredient.

There are also a number of other ingredients that establish the distinctiveness of a Greek salad and set it apart from others. These include Greek olives, peperoncini (pickled peppers), a sprinkle of oregano, and robust olive oil—all in a colorful arrangement.

We have always preferred plump calamata olives to the dry, salty, wrinkled alternatives that some people favor. This is not a cardinal rule but a personal preference based on our interpretation of symbiosis, the mutually beneficial relationship between ingredients. For this same reason we do not put too many olives on a salad, striving for a delicate balance among ingredients. A Greek olive, by its very nature, dominates. As Zorba had the potential to dominate a moment, so do many of the ingredients of Greek salad threaten to take over, unless held in balance by the other ingredient personalities. Feta, strong in its own right, tempers an olive, but it, too, needs tempering by cucumber and vinegar. Peperoncini, wildly explosive in the mouth, are balanced by the tomato and feta, as they are also neutralized by the bland but refreshing lettuce. Greek salad, like the culture from which it derives, is a study of extremes held in balance.

There are many versions of Greek salad but our intent, as with so much of the food we served at Brother Juniper's, was to capture a spirit and render it in local terms. We are, after all, not Greeks but Americans serving other Americans who want to experience not only Greek salad, per se, but the spirit behind it. The level of satisfaction sought by our patrons, and the hunger we wished to feed, was for an experience, not just a flavor. Flavors, however, are very effective in evoking memories, which are images on the soul.

When someone goes into a restaurant and orders Greek salad that person usually is not thinking about Greece, or Greek culture, or a particular part of the ancient Macedonian empire. Occasionally someone did order Greek salad because he or she had visited Greece or the Middle East and wanted to relive a memory, but most of our customers had never been to Greece and, therefore, were not performing a conscious act of correlating Greek salad to Greece. To most people it is simply a menu item—greeksalad; not much different from meatloafandmashedpotatoes. These are just things, one word things, that we eat. But, as anyone who has visited Mount Athos knows, life does not exist on one level only and everything is connected to everything else. More important, as the monks teach, the spirit of a thing is more real than the physicality of it. In that light, a bowl of Greek salad can be a form of pilgrimage, an exploration into the spirit of a culture. Though there is no Greek salad on Mount Athos there is a little of Mount Athos in all Greek salad.

How to Make Greek Salad

There are two keys to making a good Greek salad: the salad itself and the dressing.

What enlivens the dressing is the blending of olives, feta, onion, and garlic into the oil, lemon, and vinegar. This reinforces and heightens the flavors of the salad while tempering the extremes of the individual ingredients. It is a kind of homeopathic cookery, like unto like.

The actual composition of the salad—how it is arranged—allows for creativity. It can either be set up on individual plates or on a large platter from which everyone serves themselves. The usual pattern is to arrange a bed of lettuce, then to garnish it with the other ingredients. At Brother Juniper's Café we followed a basic symmetrical design: a tomato and cucumber slice in all four corners with a Greek olive next to it. We then placed two peperoncini on the platter, and sprinkled a small amount of thinly sliced red onion over the top. In the center of the salad we put some crumbled feta. The dressing was then drizzled over the whole salad and sprinkled with a pinch of oregano.

I have seen other arrangements that work as nicely as ours did. You can put all of one ingredient in a corner and design the salad by ingredient quadrants: all the tomatoes in one corner, the peperoncini in another, and the olives in another. The possibilities are endless. Regardless of the design, the flavors are ultimately brought together by the dressing and it is here that Greek salad becomes a memorable, almost transcendent, experience.

❧ Greek Salad

SERVES 8

1 large or 2 small heads fresh lettuce, such as Romaine, green leaf, red leaf, or any combination, or *mesclun* (see *Mesclun Is Not a Drug*, page 54)
4 tomatoes, each cut into 8 wedges

½ red onion, thinly sliced
32 Greek olives, preferably Calamata
1 pound feta cheese, crumbled
1 cucumber, peeled and cut into 32 slices
16 peperoncini (pickled peppers)
1 recipe Greek Salad Dressing (recipe follows)
8 pinches of dried oregano

Assemble the ingredients as described above or create your own pattern. Like most other salads, this can be mixed as one large salad, then tossed, but my preference is to arrange it on individual plates. Drizzle the dressing over the top and sprinkle the oregano over all.

🐚 Greek Salad Dressing

MAKES 3 CUPS, ENOUGH FOR 8 SERVINGS

1 cup extra-virgin olive oil (Calamata if available,
   otherwise any brand)
⅓ cup red wine vinegar
⅓ cup fresh lemon juice
¼ cup Greek Calamata olive brine
14 pitted Greek Calamata olives
3 large cloves fresh garlic
¾ cup crumbled feta cheese
¼ medium onion
¼ teaspoon whole peppercorns
¼ teaspoon dried oregano

Purée all the ingredients except the oregano in a blender or food processor until smooth. Stir in the oregano. Store unused dressing, covered, in the refrigerator. It will keep for up to 2 weeks.

Not with Hearts of Lettuce

When I was a child growing up on the outskirts of Philadelphia in the late 1950s and early 1960s, my mother often took me to Horn & Hardart for lunch. Our local branch did not feature an automat, like the one in New York City. It was, however, considered to be the archetype of home-style cooking: a place to get a decent meal at a decent price, with no frills. There are only a few things I remember about the place. One is the tapioca pudding, which was the big ball kind, each gelatinous globule smothered in a sweet vanilla custard sauce, which popped in your mouth like giant caviar. Another was the Salisbury steak that first put in motion my ongoing suspicion of menu items that sound much better than they taste. Who was to know that Salisbury steak simply referred to a meat loaf/hamburger mutation covered by brown gravy with red flecks in it?

There was also something called "hearts of lettuce with Thousand Island dressing." This is my first known memory of either term. Thousand Island dressing sounds to a child who has no prior bias or association with the name like the most wonderfully exotic sauce imaginable. Where in the world are there a thousand islands and why did they make this dressing? Hearts of lettuce, to a first-timer, sounds like the best, tenderest section of each leaf, so buttery it will just melt in your mouth. How could any rookie know that all it meant was a wedge of iceberg lettuce smothered in mayonnaise with ketchup and pickle relish? More amazingly, and I look back in sheer bewilderment at this irrational behavior, why would anyone (and I embarrassingly include myself) order this every time, even after discovering what it was? My surreal recollection is of dozens of people, adults, kids, men, and women, all ordering hearts of lettuce with Thousand Island dressing, eating half of it, and pushing the rest to the edge of the table as we prepared to attack our Salisbury steak that came with boiled green beans and mashed potatoes (with a small dent in the top so the melted patty of butter could shimmer as if it, too, were one of the thousand islands). Yes, what an image of lost youth!

Through the years I discovered a number of decent uses for Thousand Island dressing, but very few for hearts of lettuce. Thousand Island dressing is wonderful, for instance, on a corned beef sandwich. If you leave out the relish you can call it "Russian dressing," but no one ever explained to me why. As things go around and then come around, I must say that at Brother Juniper's Café we developed quite a following for Chef Salad with Thousand Island Dressing, though I am proud to say that we never attempted to foist Salisbury steak—or hearts of lettuce—on anyone.

Chef salad is a great name for a salad because it can mean almost anything. In fact, chef salad has come to be known as a kitchen sink salad; almost anything can be found in it. If you question an establishment on what is in it, the reply is, "Well, that's what comes in a chef salad—whatever the chef feels like putting in." Susan and I settled on a combination of ingredients culled from years of serving it to our community on "salad" day. It was what you might assemble if you went to a salad bar: a bed of lettuce (we did not use iceberg in favor of green leaf or red leaf), a little grated carrot, some grated Cheddar cheese, a few peperoncini, three slices of hard-boiled egg, a small amount of grated beets, four tomato wedges or cherry tomatoes, a smattering of sliced purple onion, three or four black olives, plenty of dressing (usually Thousand Island, but a few people preferred blue cheese, ranch, or oil and vinegar), a sprinkling of toasted sunflower seeds, a small poof of alfalfa sprouts, some real or imitation bacon bits, julienned ham slices (optional), and a few croutons on top. This, I considered, classic chef salad.

This salad is the perfect medium for Thousand Island dressing, but ours was so good you could eat it with a spoon. Apologies to Horn & Hardart, but there is Thousand Island dressing and there is *Thousand Island dressing*. We made the latter.

ঽ Thousand Island Dressing

MAKES 4½ CUPS

2½ cups mayonnaise, preferably Best Foods or Hellmann's
1¼ cups catsup (Heinz is still the best)
½ cup dill pickle, diced (or dill pickle relish)
¼ cup diced red onion
¼ cup diced celery
2 hard-boiled eggs, crumbled
2 cloves fresh garlic, minced
1 teaspoon dried dill weed
½ teaspoon freshly ground black pepper

Man Can Live by
Caesar Salad Alone

ʗ The preeminent culinary achievement of my youth, and the one that has had the most profound effect upon my future, was the making of Caesar salad. No other food, not even barbecue, chili, or bread, has exerted as much influence on me.

The first time I remember having Caesar salad was at Geno's Restaurant on Walnut Street in Philadelphia, about thirty years ago. Geno's was owned by a friend of the family, Gene Beechman. He had grown up with my father and performed in many musical productions my dad and his friends staged throughout the years. Though some of those friends went on to illustrious and not-so-illustrious careers in Hollywood, most of them could not afford to risk everything. So they remained behind and went into various businesses, performing locally whenever the opportunity presented itself and lamenting the stardom that would never be. Gene had a wonderful baritone voice and decided, after pursuing other ventures, that an after-theater restaurant would be the ideal showcase for his musical and culinary talents, not the least of which was making a perfect Caesar salad.

My folks talked about the restaurant so much that I finally convinced them to take me. It was a wonderful place with celebrity photos on the walls, a grand piano, and a buzz in the air as I imagined there would be in New York City on opening night of a new Broadway show. Gene or his business partner Jack would personally make the Caesar salad at each table. It was the first time I experienced restaurant as theater. After he had made all the salads, Gene disappeared for a few minutes, reappeared in a dinner jacket, struck a majestic pose in the midst of all the hub-bub, smiled sublimely, then belted out half a dozen songs from musical comedies and opera. For him, I am sure, those moments were bliss. As for me, I was already deeply lost in a taste experience beyond anything I had known. The Caesar salad had captured me; Gene's voice seemed a mile away. While my focus zoomed to the plate in front of me, the laughing, happy patrons created a cacophonous Noel Coward–like atmosphere. At the age of twelve I had my first culinary awakening.

This kind of initiation is not exactly what the spiritual elders have in mind when they speak of the transmission of knowledge. It was, however, a cosmopolitan equivalent and quite consistent with the context of my family's life. Show business and good food were an important part of the gestalt of my growing up. Caesar salad planted itself on my consciousness with all the intensity of other childhood initiations, such as first and second teeth, a first bicycle ride without training wheels, puberty, diving off the high board, that first kiss, and all the other firsts that become milestones of growing up. Perhaps it was the alchemy of the environment, the timing, the music, the sheer theatricality of it all, but somehow I became so taken with Caesar salad that I ate it at least twice a week till going off to college. One of my few after-school chores, happily rendered, was the making of the salad dressing for the evening's Caesar.

When I was twenty, I went vagabonding around the country. I "crashed" one night in a hippie enclave in Trubuco Canyon near Laguna Beach, California. It was 1970, the flower era was in its final bloom and many people of my age were discovering exotic nourishables like tofu, bean sprouts, granola, herbal teas, and whole grain breads. It was very fashionable in communes to grow your own vegetables and on this evening the little garden had lots of Romaine lettuce ready to pick. Everybody pitched in, so I volunteered to make the salad, asking only for time to run to the store to pick up a few things for the dressing. I bought a can of anchovies, some lemons, a small bottle of olive oil, and all the other necessary ingredients except garlic. There was quite a bit already hanging all over the kitchen.

Back in the commune I put together the Caesar salad and served it, along with the veggie burgers and whatever else had been prepared. The response showed the awesome power of Caesar salad to win over hearts and minds. For one night I was king of the commune. Had I wanted, I could have moved in with full tenure. That was a tempting proposition to an East Coast guy who had never even been skinny-dipping. But I decided to move on, taking my salad on the road to play other venues.

I mellowed over the years, bringing out the salad only at auspicious moments. Eventually I became a cook in our Order and discovered some Caesar salad compadres. Many of us, I learned, had similar tastes and food passions. Garlic was especially popular in our community and various people took turns making Caesar salad for special events. The challenge was to see how far one could push the use of garlic before somebody complained of an overdose. There were also several approaches to making croutons and many serious discussions took place about crouton technique.

Another debate involved batch size. There were some who would only make one bowl of dressing at a time, enough for about eight servings. Others, like me, subscribed to the blender theory, making all the dressing at once and then tossing it on a large bowl of Romaine so that everyone could eat at the same time (we would sometimes be serving fifty or more people).

This was an especially interesting dialectic, occurring as it did in a religious, semimonastic community. The importance of these discussions, I think, had quite a bit to do with the idea of viewing meals as a form of communion and as an act of ministry. In a traditional monastery there is little emphasis on the taste of food. It is simply a necessary vehicle for keeping the body alive to continue a life of prayer and worship. As one moves further from the monastery walls, the priorities change and prayer through activity becomes the challenge. The art and craft of the spiritual life is in building bridges through the things of this world until they disappear into the mystic. There are many ways to feed the soul. Our community was interested in exploring all of them.

During this Caesar salad golden era Susan was the cook at our retreat center, where I also lived and worked. She made the best Caesar salad I had ever had. She used so much garlic I cried. I am not saying that this is the reason, but I asked her to marry me. Shortly after that, we opened Brother Juniper's.

One key to Susan's Caesar is her commitment to croutons. She tosses them with both melted butter and olive oil, plenty of granulated garlic powder, and then toasts them in the oven. The result is a crisp, buttery crouton with a tender center that has a wonderful capacity to soak up dressing. When coupled with some of her other techniques, such as rubbing the bowl with a clove of garlic, adding a dash of Tabasco to the dressing, and using only freshly grated Parmesan or Pecorino Romano cheese, the result is so magnificent it can bring a grown man to his knees (as the ring on my finger proves).

We have had fine Caesars at many restaurants and friends' homes. The entire country is discovering Caesar salad, though most chain restaurants serve bottled, toned-down, disappointing versions, thus lowering expectations.

Happily, there are also some exciting variations and style developments worth noting. A recent trend is the use of whole lettuce leaves, rather than torn, which employs the heart of the Romaine. The uniform leaves are arranged creatively on the plate, with croutons artistically placed, and they can be picked up and eaten out-of-hand. *Frisée,* an endive-like lettuce, is also showing up in Caesar salads, probably because it traps the dressing in its feathery, slightly bitter tendrils. (For this reason it should be used sparingly, in conjunction with Romaine, but never as the only green; otherwise it gets soggy with dressing.)

Croutons, too, have been undergoing a renaissance of design. One delicious variation includes searing some anchovy and cheese directly into them.

Grilled chicken is finding its way into many Caesar salads. Other nontraditional ingredients such as tomatoes and cucumbers are also being tried. There is nothing wrong with these innovations. Problems occur only when these additions become more important than the dressing.

Caesar salad, more than most other salads, is dependent upon its dressing. The lettuce and croutons in a Caesar salad are, for better or worse, merely a backdrop for the most exciting flavor burst the palate can endure. If Caesar Cardini, as the legend goes, created this salad in Tijuana during a moment of creative desperation, he surely belongs in the culinary hall of fame and, as far as I'm concerned, in the pantheon of lesser saints.

We have had many people tell us that our Caesar salad was the best they ever tasted. This never surprised me because I was already convinced. I have also been to many other places where they boast, "This is the best Caesar salad you will ever have." Can we all be right?

There were a few key items on our menu that brought people back and caused them to have a deeper connection with us. Bread was one of them, barbecue another. The Greek salad had a following almost as passionate as the Caesar. Our chili also evoked an intense response. In retrospect, it appears that the common thread was the passion and devotion invested in each of them. These are foods that are connected not only to memories but to initiations of consciousness. We all have them and, strangely, even in this melting pot of postmodern America, we may share quite a few. If there is, as I believe, such a thing as a uniquely American soul quality, it surely reflects in our shared passion for bread, chili, barbecue, and recently but most definitely, Caesar salad.

How to Make Great Caesar Salad

Here are a few tips we learned along the way:

· Wash and dry the lettuce thoroughly. Wet leaves dilute the dressing.

· It does not matter whether you cut or tear the leaves (personal preference prevails), but bigger pieces make a more elegant presentation.

· Croutons should not be bone dry or rock hard. It defeats the purpose to have the crouton so crisp that it retains its independent identity. It should be considered a vehicle for an artistic sop. Toss some croutons in the dressing for a few seconds to prime them, reserving a few for garnishing the top when serving. The best croutons are those made just before assembling the salad. Save the extras in a freezer bag and either put them in the freezer or use within two to three days. They also make great snacks.

· The theatrical way to make the dressing is, of course, in the bowl, at the table. However, I find no loss of flavor when I make the dressing in a blender and pour it over the salad when serving time arrives. Blender dressing can last for a week in the refrigerator, though the anchovy flavor gets stronger each day.

· Should the egg be coddled? Should it coat the leaves first, before the dressing, or may it be added to the dressing? These are questions that have been debated ever since St. Cardini. Susan and I have seriously grappled with them and have finally arrived at a consensus—coddling and then whizzing the egg in the blender is best. The main reason in its favor is that coddling eliminates the sliminess inherent in a raw egg, while still maintaining the emulsifying and coating properties of the uncooked egg.* Pour the coddled egg over the leaves and toss, then add the dressing.

Another option is to blend the coddled egg into the dressing, which makes for a creamy combination, one that still has the capacity to coat the leaves thoroughly. You may also simply leave the egg out.

· Always use freshly grated Parmesan or Romano cheese. Avoid using the pregrated stuff in jars unless there is no possible way to get your hands on the real thing. There is absolutely no comparison.

· Do not throw the leftover salad away. Second-day Caesar (which I call Wilted Caesar), is its own art form—but not for the squeamish.

---

*To coddle an egg, first pierce the broad end with a pin or needle. Then on a spoon lower the egg into a pan of boiling water and boil for exactly one minute. Remove immediately and plunge the egg into a bowl of cold water to stop the cooking process.

🐌 Caesar Salad

4 LARGE OR 8 SMALL SERVINGS

For the Salad

2 heads Romaine lettuce (you can add a little *frisée* or fancy
leaf lettuce, but Romaine is traditional), washed, dried, and
torn into medium-sized pieces
2 cups Croutons (page 37)
1 cup freshly grated Parmesan or Romano cheese
      Caesar Salad Dressing (makes about 2½ cups;
      use all or part, according to taste)
1 tablespoon finely minced anchovy (about 2 anchovies) or
      1 tablespoon anchovy paste
5 large cloves fresh garlic, minced
1½ cups extra-virgin olive oil
3 tablespoons red wine vinegar
1 teaspoon Worcestershire sauce
¼ teaspoon freshly ground black pepper
¼ teaspoon hot pepper sauce (Tabasco or other)
½ teaspoon prepared Dijon-style mustard or
      ⅛ teaspoon mustard powder
¼ cup fresh lemon juice, strained
¼ cup freshly grated Parmesan or Romano cheese
1 egg, coddled (see above)

Have all the salad ingredients ready.

Make the Caesar salad dressing:

Blender method—Put all the ingredients in a blender and
process until smooth.

Theatrical method—Rub the inside of a wooden salad bowl
with a crushed fresh garlic clove. With a fork or whisk, mix the
remaining ingredients in the bowl, beginning with the anchovy

and garlic and gradually working in each of the others except the egg. Proceed as described below.

To dress and serve the salad: If using blender-made dressing (with the egg already blended in), combine all the salad ingredients in a salad bowl and toss with the desired amount of dressing.

If using the **theatrical** method, make the dressing as described above, directly in the salad bowl. Add the croutons to the bowl and toss in the dressing. In a separate bowl, whisk or blend the egg, then pour it over the lettuce in a bowl and toss. Add the egg-tossed lettuce to the salad bowl and toss with the dressing and croutons. Sprinkle the grated cheese over the top and serve. You may also shave thin pieces of the cheese with a wire cheese slicer or a potato peeler over the top of the salad. This adds a nice artistic touch to the presentation.

N O T E : Our good friends Steve and Nanette Garner, who make an exceptional Caesar salad of their own, taught us a terrific garlic trick. They use roasted garlic (see page 172 for directions), which allows them to use more without the usual garlic burn. In order to maximize flavor they still use 1 clove of fresh garlic for every 8 cloves of roasted. If you want to try this substitution, use the full amount (8 roasted, 1 fresh) to replace the 5 cloves of fresh garlic listed above.

?ふ The Best Croutons

MAKES A LOT—11 CUPS

1 One-pound loaf French or sourdough bread
½ pound unsalted butter

½ cup olive oil

4 tablespoons coarse garlic powder, also called granulated
garlic (This works better than fresh garlic as it gives the
croutons more garlic flavor.)

Cut the bread into ¾-inch cubes and put in a large bowl.

Melt the butter and olive oil over medium heat. Add the
granulated garlic. Pour the mixture over the fresh bread cubes,
tossing well to coat.

Spread the bread cubes on a baking sheet and bake at 350
degrees (300 degrees if using a convection oven) for 25 to 30
minutes, stirring occasionally so they brown evenly. Do not
overbake; allow the center of the croutons to remain slightly soft.

Cool and use. Store the extra croutons in freezer bags, at
room temperature, for up to 1 week. They can also be kept in the
freezer for months.

Tabbouleh and the

Lineage of Noah

૨ঌ When I travelled throughout Israel with my parents and youngest brother a few years ago there were certain foods that consistently sustained us. My brother Harry went absolutely bonkers over the hummus, a smooth paste made from chickpeas, tahini (sesame paste), lemon juice, garlic, and olive oil.

Israelis eat lots of olive oil and garlic; the cuisine is not unlike Greek or other Middle Eastern foods. Everywhere one goes there is tabbouleh, a parsley and cracked wheat salad dressed in olive oil, lemon juice, mint, and garlic. While my brother gorged himself on hummus, I did the same with tabbouleh. Between us, there was enough garlic breath to support an entire mouthwash industry.

When I returned to the States, back to my community in California where tabbouleh was often served, I realized that American-style tabbouleh had the proportions wrong. Bulgur, or parboiled cracked wheat, is not the first ingredient in authentic tabbouleh—parsley is. Tabbouleh is actually a parsley salad, which is great for us symbiosis freaks who understand that the more parsley in a dish the greater the capacity for garlic.

On the other hand, parsley salad can run through the system pretty quickly, leaving behind an empty, hungry feeling. The bulgur provides enough bulk and complex carbohydrates to provide ballast.

Susan and I have had many discussions and played with a number of different combinations, looking for the right balance of grain and parsley. Our quest for the perfect tabbouleh falls right in with our other culinary pilgrimages—barbecue sauce, chili, Caesar salad, and on and on. We have tried tabbouleh in almost every local restaurant that dares to make it. Every time we have it the recipe discussion reopens, followed soon thereafter at home by another experimental version by Susan, and then a debate about the lineage of Noah.

Susan has the ability to consume herself in a quest. One night, before we were married, I walked into the library of our retreat center and found her surrounded by books. There were three different translations of the Bible, commentaries by Old Testament scholars, atlases, archaeological journals, history books, and her notebook. She had discovered a discrepancy in two different Old Testament accounts of the lineage of Noah. Down some long corridor in her mind, Susan saw that the implications of this discrepancy could affect our understanding of both the Old and New Testaments. If she could only reconcile the contradiction, then everything would be clear, wouldn't it?

I do not know. The flash of intuition at the end of that corridor was too far away for me, or blinking in a fashion only Susan could fathom. Correlation is the key to any pilgrimage—she was onto something that was about to connect things for her. This kind of connecting is at the heart of what could be called a religious experience. She was definitely having one. Her face was all lit up, flush with the excitement of the quest. She was Indiana Jones, close to finding the Holy Grail. Her brilliance was blinding; I could not stay in the same room, could not help her. It was her quest, and hers alone.

To this day I do not understand what we now reverently call

"Susan's quest for the lineage of Noah." After a few days the corridor narrowed, the flash at the end, which she so feverishly tried to correlate through her study, began to fade, like a great dream that seems less compelling after a few days. Every now and then, usually after a bowl of tabbouleh, we pull out the Bible and try to re-create the convergence of thoughts that thrust her into her illumined state that night, but Noah and his boys, like slippery mythological phantoms, keep slipping out of the noose.

Due to a curious bend in the road, some of that same zeal now gets channeled into our food quests. Though we consider ourselves protectors of authenticity and tradition, we also believe in the neotraditional ethic: Honor the past but make it contemporary. The following recipe is the culmination of Susan's persistent quest for the perfect tabbouleh.

ン Tabbouleh

SERVES 2 TO 4

½ cup uncooked bulgur wheat
1½ cups water
3 bunches parsley, washed, stemmed, and coarsely chopped
1 large bunch peppermint (spearmint is too strong), washed, stemmed, and coarsely chopped
8 cloves garlic, peeled and coarsely chopped
1 medium red onion, diced
1 large cucumber, peeled, seeded, and diced
1 large tomato, chopped into bite-sized pieces
6 peperoncini (pickled peppers), stemmed and coarsely chopped
½ cup fresh lemon juice

¾ cup extra-virgin olive oil
1 teaspoon salt
½ pound feta cheese, crumbled

In a dry frying pan, toast the bulgur over medium-high heat until it begins to crackle and pop, stirring constantly to prevent burning. When the grain appears to turn a little browner (it starts out as a light brown), remove the pan from the heat.

Bring the water to a boil in a small pan. Turn off the heat and stir in the toasted bulgur. Cover and let it sit for 30 minutes, or until all the water is absorbed. Transfer the cooked bulgur to a mixing bowl.

In a food processor, pulse the parsley, peppermint, and garlic in batches until finely chopped, but not creamed or puréed. You may also mince them by hand. (Do not pack the processor too full or you will have an uneven mixture.)

Combine the parsley/mint/garlic mixture with the bulgur. Add the remaining ingredients, toss well, and refrigerate, covered, for 1 hour before serving.

Hummus and the

Magical Halvah

ેઢ There is an old Sufi story about a young man in search of the mysteries and meaning of life, who survived his travails by nourishing himself with a magical halvah. He found it in a river bed every morning and it tasted so divine that he was certain it had been sent to him by Allah. He was so energized by this paste of sesame, almond, pistachio, and honey that he developed super strength and wisdom and overcame all obstacles, and even married a beautiful princess who lived in a palace above the river. After he married her he discovered, to his embarrassment, that the halvah was, in actuality, makeup that his princess bride scraped off her face every night and flushed into the river as garbage.

There are many ways to interpret such a tale and I will attempt none (the Sufis, a mystical branch of Islam, usually ascribe at least four levels of interpretation to every story). I retell it only because it reminds me of the first time I ever had hummus, that wonderful creamy chickpea salad/dip with garlic, lemon, olive oil, and tahini (sesame paste). I was only thirteen years old and my parents decided to take me and my brother Fred, who was eleven, to a restaurant in South Philly called The Middle East. It was a night of many firsts.

The tastes and images of that night fall into a category that most people would call exotic. This was a time long before *gyros, souvlaki,* and *falafel* were part of the American culinary lexicon. Philadelphia in 1963, to my knowledge, had only this one restaurant featuring two distinct Middle Eastern delicacies: hummus and belly dancing. The taste of rosewater, which appeared in many of the dishes, was a brand new sensation to my virginal palate; like mystical attar it transported me out of South Philly to an interior place where magic carpets seemed, somehow, viable. But, it was the hummus that blew me away.

I think my brother Fred's lingering memory of that night is probably of the belly dancing, though he might deny it today. I must admit that the well-endowed women performing their symbolic gyrations not three feet from where I was shoveling hummus-slathered pita pieces into my mouth left some indelible impressions on my psyche. Not the dancing or the *dolmas* (stuffed grape leaves), or the baba ghanouj (eggplant dip), or even the shish kebab, on that exotic Alladin-like night, left an impression as deep as the hummus.

During the past ten years, hummus, like so many other ethnic foods, has become almost mainstream food for many Americans, especially for vegetarians as they look for a rich and filling protein substitute. Sadly, during this boom I have been exposed to too much mediocre hummus: grainy or lumpy, too dry, too sweet, or just boring. I think I have become jaded and cynical. I hesitate to order it unless somebody can first vouch for it. Occasionally, though, I run into the real thing: smooth and creamy, tart, not too heavy on the sesame paste, with a little pool of high-quality olive oil floating on top. At those times, when I find it, like a gift from Allah, I feel like the young Sufi man and his magical halvah—undaunted, again inspired to face the challenges of life and to seek out its mysteries, despite the consequences.

₹ Hummus

MAKES 2 CUPS

¼ cup white sesame seeds
¼ cup extra-virgin olive oil, plus about 1 tablespoon for
  optional garnish
1½ cups (15-ounce can) cooked chickpeas (garbanzo beans),
  drained, reserving the liquid for use as needed*
8–10 large cloves fresh or roasted garlic
½ cup fresh lemon juice
½–1 teaspoon salt, to taste

Toast the sesame seeds in a dry frying pan, stirring constantly, until they begin to pop, crackle, and lightly brown. In a food processor or blender blend the seeds with the olive oil until a smooth paste or butter is formed.

Add the chickpeas, garlic, and lemon juice and blend until smooth. Add chickpea liquid, as needed, to attain a creamy texture. Add salt to taste.

Serve the hummus on a platter with crackers or pita bread. You can make an indentation in the top of the hummus and drizzle a small amount of extra-virgin olive oil into the well, for that special Middle Eastern touch.

---

*To prepare chickpeas from scratch, soak 1 cup of dry chickpeas in 2 cups of cold water for a minimum of 4 hours, or overnight. Drain and discard any remaining water. In a pot, mix the beans with 2 cups of fresh cold water. Cover and bring to a boil, simmering for one hour or until the chickpeas are soft. Drain and cool, saving the leftover water. Measure the cooked beans per the recipe.

Baba Ghanouj and the

Temple of Mount Moriah

❧ As mentioned in the chapter on tabbouleh (page 39), I once spent three weeks traveling throughout Israel with my parents and one of my brothers. My father, a good Jew and loyal supporter of the State of Israel, wanted to see where his trees were planted, while each of us had our own interior agendas.

We visited Bethlehem and the grotto where the birth of Jesus is commemorated. We traveled through Nazareth, an agriculturally rich region that reminded me very much of Sonoma County, California. I walked the Via Dolorosa, retracing the steps of Jesus, leading to Golgotha and crucifixion. My Dad and I explored the mountain fort of Masada, where a small band of Jews, fleeing from the final destruction of the Temple, held off the Roman army for months and then years. I even floated like a bobbing cork in the Dead Sea and walked around the ruins of Jericho.

But the most memorable event occurred when I broke away from my family, leaving them at the Wailing Wall, and entered the Mosque of Omar, also known as the Dome of the Rock. I believe that this site, on what is called Mount Moriah, can rightly be considered the center of the universe, at least as far as Christians, Muslims, and Jews are concerned.

It was here that Abraham offered his son Isaac in sacrifice, gratefully accepting God's reprieve at the last moment, thus entering into one of many covenants with his Creator.

It was also here that King Solomon built the first magnificent Temple, and where King Herod later built his own version, thinking it would establish him as the Messiah. A few years later Jesus came and threw the money lenders out of Herod's Temple, demanding purification, which ultimately resulted in his death and, as Christians believe, his resurrection.

Many centuries later, Mohammed hid in a building just across from the Temple ruins, later supposedly ascending to heaven on a horse from the very rock upon which Abraham offered up Isaac.

When the Muslims took control of Jerusalem, which means "the city of peace," a caliph named Omar built a mosque with a beautiful golden dome over the rock and for centuries only Muslims could enter. When Jerusalem was partitioned in 1948, the Muslims were allowed to keep the mosque but it was opened to visitors of other faiths during certain hours. Only Muslims, however, are allowed to pray there.

As I walked around the rock of Mount Moriah, which is protected from pilgrims by a fence, this incredible history unfolded in my mind. As a Jewish Christian I felt directly connected to at least two-thirds of the four-thousand-year heritage within my grasp. I tried to visualize the many important dramas that had taken place there. With a number of Islamic pilgrims kneeling around me, offering their thanks to Allah, a strong desire to pray overcame me. I closed my eyes and offered a prayer of peace and unity to the One God who seemed to have sprung from this rock.

Then a strange thing happened. A security guard approached, wagging his finger in chastisement and said, "No, no, no, you must not pray. Only Muslims may pray here."

"Same God," I said.

"I am sorry," he sincerely replied. "It is the rules of the management."

I pondered his interesting choice of words and continued to walk around the rock. When he was out of sight I gave in, again, to the overpowering sense of divine mystery in the air, and closed my eyes in prayer. Within seconds he was all over me like a mad hornet.

"I warned you not to pray in here! Now you must leave."

"Do I understand you correctly?" I asked, incredulous. "Are you throwing me out of the Temple of God for praying?"

"Yes, and you must go now, this very minute!"

I found myself standing outside the Mosque of Omar, shaking my head at the amazing irony. Looking up I demanded, "How can you allow this? This is nuts!"

Then I had an experience I will never forget. My body and mind filled with peace and, for just a quick moment, I saw this scene as if from an aerial view, maybe through the eyes of God (who could say?). I saw all of us, adults acting like children, squabbling over prayer rights to holy places, fighting over land rights to ancestral ground, and making war with other humans in the name of the God we all profess to love. We were all children, together, fighting in a big sandbox, and suddenly the whole situation seemed strangely comical. "We will work it out one of these days," I heard in my mind. "Be patient. We're just kids."

Nearby was the bazaar, in what is called "the old city" of Jerusalem. As I shuffled through the maze of corridors in the bazaar, lost in the amazement of what had just happened to me at the Dome of the Rock, I found myself staring at an Arab food stand where they served platters of hummus and baba ghanouj. These two creamy condiment salads rank high on my scale of comfort foods. They are both laced with garlic, olive oil, and lemon juice that, as I review my food passions in these pages, seem like a recurrent theme of my life.

I ordered a plate of baba ghanouj, with a large round, uncut, pita bread that I tore into pieces and used as little scoopers. The baba ghanouj, with its roasted eggplant base and sesame paste seasoning, settled me down, though my heart was still thumping from the excitement of both the encounter with the security guard and my postapocalyptic vision of religious unity.

After wiping my plate clean with the last piece of pita, my stomach full, I rejoined my family, still at the Wailing Wall. I was refreshed, digesting, hopeful, feeling certain that I would one day return and be allowed to pray at the rock. It was an honor, I now realized, to be thrown out for praying in this ongoing tragi-comedy, in this Jerusalem, the city of peace.

ॐ Baba Ghanouj

SERVES 6 TO 8

2 tablespoons olive oil (for coating pan and eggplants)
2 large eggplants (2¾ pounds total)
¼ cup white sesame seeds
½ cup extra-virgin olive oil
8–10 large cloves garlic, fresh or roasted
½ cup plus 3 tablespoons fresh lemon juice
1 teaspoon salt
A few sprigs of fresh parsley for garnish

Preheat the oven to 425 degrees (375 degrees if using a convection oven). Lightly coat a baking pan with the 2 table-spoons olive oil. Pierce the eggplants all around, about ¼-inch deep, with a knife. Place them in the oiled pan, turning them around in the oil to coat. Bake on the middle shelf of the oven for approximately 35 minutes, or until the eggplants are thoroughly softened. Remove from the oven and cool. Cut off and discard the stems. Coarsely chop the eggplant (including the skin), place it in a bowl, and set aside.

In a dry pan, toast the sesame seeds, stirring constantly, till they crackle, pop, and begin to brown. In a blender or food processor combine the extra-virgin olive oil with the sesame seeds and blend to a paste.

Add the eggplant, garlic, lemon juice, and salt. Blend till smooth and creamy. Remove the mixture to a serving bowl and refrigerate for 1 hour. Garnish with the parsley sprigs and serve with pieces of pita bread for dipping.

Putting Out the Fire of Desire

❧ In the early days of our brotherhood, around 1968, there were a number of fiery characters who came through our door. Father Paul Blighton, the founder of the Order, used to put some of the more hot-tempered brothers on a blue cheese diet. He claimed that blue cheese "puts out the fire."

Throughout history there have always been popular theories regarding the magical properties of ordinary foods. In contemporary literature, for example, Laura Esquivel has revitalized this romantic view in her popular novel (and film), *Like Water for Chocolate.*

Father Paul had a healthy respect for the symbolic values of things. When he said blue cheese "puts out the fire," he was speaking from a shamanistic tradition of interpretation; a metaphorical and metaphysical viewpoint in which every temperament has corresponding antidotes and counterbalances. Dr. Samuel Hahnemann worked from similiar theories in developing classical homeopathy. Herbalists and naturopaths, as well as Oriental healers such as acupuncturists, also follow complete cosmolgical systems in which seemingly eccentric applications make sense. It is the context that counts, always.

Every restaurant, whether consciously or not, subscribes to its own context. When a customer enters the doors of an establishment, a universe of assumptions is handed out with the menu. Most restaurants conform to the prevailing winds of the mass mind in which nobody thinks twice about their assumptions. But as the trend toward more conscious eating grows, we find people asking questions such as, "Is there any dairy or oil in this dish?" or "Is this a free-range chicken?" A health-oriented cosmology, not to be confused with a spiritual or mythopoetical one, is emerging. With the exception of a few macrobiotic restaurants, customers do not generally ask, "Was this soup stirred clockwise or counterclockwise?" but more and more people do want to be conscious of what it is that they are eating.

I never noticed blue cheese dressing to have a particular effect on temperament. Because of the "putting out the fire" legends, however, I was sensitive to this possibility whenever anyone ordered blue cheese dressing at Brother Juniper's. We had customers who pleaded for the recipe, some who ordered it by the half-gallon, but never anyone who said, "I'm feeling particularly passionate today. Perhaps I should have the blue cheese to, you know, sort of balance me out." Nevertheless, I could not help visualizing a blanket being spread over some smoldering embers inside the psyche of everyone who ordered it, imagining that, perhaps, a child was going to be spared an unnecessary scolding, a spouse would be less angry with a mate, or a waitress might get a bigger tip, because this rich, velvety blue cheese dressing had performed some subtle magical work in addition to pleasing the palate.

ଏବ Blue Cheese Dressing

MAKES 4 CUPS
This dressing enhances any salad, but is also excellent on baked

potatoes, as a vegetable dip, as a sandwich spread, and as a dipping sauce for hot chicken wings.

2 cups sour cream (You may substitute no-fat or "lite" sour
   cream.)
1 cup mayonnaise, preferably Best Foods or Hellmann's
¾ cup crumbled blue cheese (The better the quality, the better
   the dressing.)
2 tablespoons low-fat milk
2 cloves fresh garlic, minced
1 tablespoon Worcestershire sauce, preferably Lea & Perrins
½ teaspoon freshly ground black pepper
¼ teaspoon mustard powder

Mix all the ingredients in a large bowl, whisking until creamy. If too thick, add a little more milk. The consistency should be thick enough to hold a mixing spoon straight upright.

Allow the dressing to sit for at least 1 hour for the flavors to blend. Adjust the texture, if necessary, with more milk. Cover and refrigerate. It will keep for up to 1 week.

Mesclun Is Not a Drug

❧ Doug Gosling is an extraordinary gardener. For a number of years he grew a business called The Farallones Gardens, in the hills of Occidental, about fifteen miles from Forestville. Initially, this was part of a larger project, an experimental community devoted to the teaching and implementation of appropriate technology in developing nations. Besides the gardens, there were energy-efficient houses, composting toilets, water reclamation systems, passive solar energy panels, and many other "living lightly" and "sustainable society" experiments. The Farallones Institute no longer exists and, sadly, neither does Doug's garden.

Doug is an elfin character, almost a nature spirit. He was the first to introduce me to *mesclun,* back in 1986. "What did you call it?" I asked suspiciously, thinking he was trying to sell me a psychotropic drug.

"*Mesclun,* it's a blend of unusual wild greens that supplement lettuce and add some interesting flavors to your salad."

Doug then brought out a plastic bag full of odd-shaped green, red, and gold leafy vegetables with names like *mâche, mizuna,* red kale, calendula petals, and *arugula.* Unlike lettuce, which is usually harvested by the head, the leaves had been clipped from plants and bushes that would continue to grow, producing more for the next day. Every few days Doug sent us a big bag of *mesclun* and fresh herbs, which we then mixed with regular green and red leaf lettuce, producing one of the most beautiful and delicious salads imaginable. Since that time the "wild greens" salad has become a standard item in restaurants across the country. There are small organic gardens throughout Sonoma County that ship *mesclun* blends all over America. One of our local gardens ships boxes of *mesclun* to Hawaii, where, to my surprise, the climate is not quite right for growing such a diversity of greens.

We are fortunate to live in Sonoma County, an area designated by Luther Burbank as the most perfect agricultural region in the world. Because of this good fortune we have witnessed a number of culinary trends in their early formation. We have had the opportunity to meet some of the finest chefs in the world, watching them smack their lips at the bounty with which they can create exciting dishes with the local produce.

Our ambition at Brother Juniper's was not on a grand culinary scale, but access to the world's finest ingredients did allow us to prepare some dishes that would be considered gourmet fare in other parts of the country. There were times, for example, when we served an ear of fresh white corn on a popsicle stick for one dollar that we would later see featured (without the stick) for four or five dollars at a fancy restaurant.

Spring salad, which is what we called the *mesclun* and lettuce blend, became a featured item, changing with the seasons as different wild greens came into harvest. Susan felt that it was important to create a special dressing for this salad to complement and showcase the various flavors. The base is balsamic vinegar, another pantry item now popular but not so well known back in 1986. She blended it with olive oil, capers, and a few other things to create our Spring Salad Caper Dressing.

Mesclun mixes are now available in supermarkets across the country. If yours does not carry it, go boldly to the produce manager and ask him for it. When he looks at you funny, feel free to look him back, straight in the eye, and tell him, "*Mesclun,* my friend, is not a drug."

❧ Spring Salad with Caper Dressing

ENOUGH FOR 2 LARGE OR 4 SMALL SALADS

1 head red leaf, green leaf, or bibb lettuce
¼ pound *mesclun* (available in most supermarkets, sometimes called "wild greens mix" or "gourmet salad blend")
¼ cup coarsley chopped fresh herbs, such as a combination of oregano, basil, thyme, lemon thyme, marjoram, tarragon, chives, or any other personal favorites
 Caper Dressing (or substitute Raspberry Vinaigrette on page 57)
½ cup extra-virgin olive oil
¼ cup balsamic vinegar
1 tablespoon fresh lemon juice
1 tablespoon whole capers with juice
1 clove garlic, chopped
⅛ teaspoon freshly ground black pepper

Wash and dry the lettuce. Tear it into large or medium pieces. In a salad bowl toss it with the *mesclun* and herbs.

Make the Caper Dressing: Purée all the ingredients in a blender until creamy.

Dress the greens lightly, just before serving. Serve on small salad plates rather than in bowls, to show off the colors and the variety of greens.

NOTE: It is important to use freshly picked herbs to heighten the flavors. In combination with the greens, the herbs provide a variety of flavor bursts that make each bite of salad unique.

❧ Raspberry Vinaigrette

MAKES 1 CUP
This dressing is also good on spinach salad, tossed garden salad, and, surprisingly, fruit salad. With the addition of a few toasted walnuts and a small amount of chèvre *(goat milk cheese), it also makes a spectacular Spring Salad variation.*

¾ cup olive or light vegetable oil
5 tablespoons red raspberry vinegar (We recommend
   Kozlowski's brand, if you can find it.)
2 tablespoons fresh lemon juice
½ shallot, minced or 1 tablespoon minced onion
1 large clove garlic, minced (omit if using on a fruit salad)
2 teaspoons sugar
½ teaspoon salt
¼ teaspoon freshly ground black pepper

In a bowl stir all the ingredients together. Do not use a blender or food processor. Store in a covered jar and refrigerate for up to 2 weeks. Shake well before using.

Bread Salad

෭෧ This is a dish Susan developed for our annual Christmas party, and people were talking about it for months after. It is a salad without lettuce and a concession to people like me who think some salads should simply be an excuse for crouton-sopping. One of the reasons I always ask for twice the amount of Caesar salad than I can eat is so that the next day I can have it wilted with the croutons softened and full of that incredibly flavorful dressing. Bread salad is a way to cut to the chase and get right to the sop.

Susan uses a variation of our Greek salad dressing, but you could use other vinaigrettes if you prefer. There are enough crunchy things in this dish to create the illusion of lettuce, but the cold hard truth is that lettuce would just get in the way.

We prefer to use our more savory breads like oreganato or Cajun three-pepper but simple French or sourdough will work fine. Just be sure to use plenty of dressing, as the bread soaks it up like a sponge, which is, after all, the whole idea.

🐦 Bread Salad

SERVES 4

¾ pound fresh or slightly stale bread (French, sourdough, oreganato, Cajun three-pepper, or any rustic peasant bread), cut into ½-inch cubes
¼ cup (about 12) Greek olives, preferably Calamata
½ medium white or red onion, chopped
½ cucumber, peeled, seeded, and chopped
1 large tomato, cut into bite-sized pieces, or ½ basket cherry tomatoes, chopped
6 peperoncini (pickled peppers), stemmed and coarsely chopped
½ cup feta cheese, crumbled
2 tablespoons chopped fresh parsley
1 teaspoon dried oregano
    Special Bread Salad Dressing (makes 1 cup)
⅓ cup extra-virgin olive oil
⅓ cup red wine vinegar
2 tablespoons Calamata olive juice
1 tablespoon peperoncini juice from the jar
2 tablespoons fresh lemon juice
4 large cloves garlic, minced

Mix all the salad ingredients, except the oregano, in a large salad bowl. Make the Special Bread Salad Dressing: In a mixing bowl stir all of the salad dressing ingredients together.

Pour the salad dressing over the salad and gently toss to distribute the dressing, taking care not to mash the bread. Sprinkle the oregano over the top and serve.

The Coleslaw Reaction

Revisited

In *Brother Juniper's Bread Book* I wrote of a phenomenon we often observed at our café. I called it "the coleslaw reaction." It usually occurred like this: A first-time customer would come in and order the barbecue platter, which consisted of either chicken, spare ribs, hot sausage, tofu, or tempeh, accompanied by a couple of slices of French bread (either white or whole wheat), a pickle, and a dish of coleslaw. The barbecue entrée was covered with our Holy Smoke sauce and, naturally, this would be the prime focus of the dish. The meal and conversation ensued normally until the first bite of coleslaw (if we were not too busy Susan and I would listen for the inevitable reaction). Whatever the topic of conversation, all talk would stop and the startled diner would blurt out, "Boy, that's good slaw!" (Chuckle, wink, slap on the arm in the kitchen as Susan and I felt justified, healed, and uplifted; again reconfirming to ourselves that there are some foods that can stop time, create an epiphany, and overcome bias and prior assumption. This revelation became a sustaining energy for us as we, otherwise, wore down through the daily grind of our efforts.)

These so-called reactions became somewhat of an obsession for me. I was always on the lookout for other occurrences. The "muffin reaction" is one that I also described in my previous book. In this one, the surprised patron, expecting the usual dry, boring muffin that has become the standard insult throughout America's breakfast restaurants, encounters a muffin that is, lo and behold, enjoyable. It does not need to be dunked or disguised with coffee or marmalade; it stands on its own as a wonderful treat. The common reaction is usually worded, "My God, this muffin is moist!"

Because of these reactions a new standard, perhaps unrealistic, exerted itself at Brother Juniper's. If a dish were merely good, but did not elicit an exclamatory outburst, we struggled with pangs of failure. Having once tasted the ego-flattering power to induce involuntary reactions, we were unfulfilled unless replicating this power every time we introduced a new menu item or product. This pattern heaped a terrible pressure upon us. A singer is only as good as his last hit, and thus is a chef entrapped by his most recent gustatory accomplishment. Therefore, simultaneous to upholding the "food reaction" standard, a new quest began to emerge: How to get off this wheel!

There were other dishes on the menu that met the requirements of the "reaction" model. Coleslaw and muffins were notable because they caught the patron unawares. Main dishes like barbecue, Neo-Texas chili, and the salad platters were expected to impress. Many people traveled from as far away as San Francisco, sixty miles, because of word-of-mouth endorsement. They expected to be awed. For these people, the importance of the unexpected was critical. Thus, the coleslaw reaction was a vital part of the magic of Brother Juniper's. Other items that stopped conversation included corn bread with whole corn (*Brother Juniper's Bread Book*, pages 106–109), Ginger Fizz (page 183 in this book), Susan's Spicy Red Salsa (page 8), and just about every type of yeasted bread that we served. These items were like supporting actors, stealing the scene from the main stars, like Jack

Lemmon in *Mr. Roberts,* Whoopi Goldberg in *Ghost,* or *Seinfeld*'s Kramer.

Getting back to coleslaw, there are some critical principles about it that I think need to be articulated. We have all had bad coleslaw, but some of us have had the great good fortune of encountering wonderful slaw. I often think of an episode of *M*A*S*H,* where Hawkeye arranges for a shipment of barbecue from everyone's favorite place, Adam's Ribs, supposedly the world's best barbecue pit. Every time a character is asked if he has heard of Adam's Ribs he says, "Oh yeah, and what about that slaw!"

Here is what I think is important and not important about coleslaw. Not important: pineapple slices, grated carrots, apples, yogurt, raisins, walnuts, and just about everything else that is supposedly part of someone's grandmother's secret world-famous recipe. Important: a small amount of fresh onion, fresh crunchy cabbage, apple cider vinegar, good-quality mayonnaise, regular granulated sugar, and fresh coarsely ground black pepper. Anything more than this is overkill and unnecessary. Coleslaw does not have to be colorful. Red cabbage works, especially the first day, but fades out and gives the dressing a funny color the second day (when the flavor of the slaw really reaches its peak). Red onion is okay because there is just a small amount used and it adds a splash of color, again fading out the second day.

The secret to good slaw is the dressing, which blends the extremes of sweet and sour (sugar and vinegar), with the richness of creamy mayonnaise. The dressing holds in suspension the pungency of the onions, cabbage, and black pepper. When properly combined, these flavors cover the full spectrum of the palate and bring a joy that induces an involuntary squeal of delight.

One day I was enjoying some barbecue and coleslaw with my friend Stephen, who was visiting from Portland, Oregon. We were discussing the feasibility of bottling our barbecue sauce, a dream that became a reality four years later. I have a vivid recollection of Stephen, his mouth painted with streaks of red, deep in the pleasure throes of Aidells Smoked Creole Sausage smothered in Holy Smoke Barbecue Sauce. We were heatedly discussing the marketing possibilities of hot, medium, and mild, when he took a forkful of coleslaw to cool off his mouth. He stopped talking for a second, wiping away a dribble of creamy dressing at the corner of his mouth, looked me in the eye, and said, "Boy, that's good slaw!"

"Stephen," I giggled, "you've just performed the classic coleslaw reaction—to the very words."

With a smile on his face he took another combination taste of barbecue followed by slaw. The red and white sauces created some interesting patterns on his lips as he quickly wiped them clean. He just kept on smiling and dove in for another taste. Our discussion was ended, the magic was working.

❧ Coleslaw

SERVES SIX

1 large head cabbage
½ cup finely diced onion (yellow, white, or red)
1½ cups good mayonnaise (Hellmann's, Best Foods, or homemade)
¼ cup apple cider vinegar
½ cup granulated white sugar
1 teaspoon coarsely ground fresh black pepper

Grate or shred the cabbage as thinly as possible. In a bowl, combine it with the diced onion and all the other ingredients.

Lemons into Lemonade;

Pasta into Pasta Salad

?❧ One of the reasons I do not spend a lot of time reminiscing about the good old days at Brother Juniper's Café is that I experienced a great deal of embarrassment and humiliation on a regular basis. Of course, the public rarely saw this side of things since most of my humiliations occurred before we opened the doors. In my own mind, though, no amount of praise for the food could completely wipe out the sense of inadequacy I regularly felt as many of my experiments or innovations flopped.

Susan, probably as a test of her love, was usually there when I made my blunders. Fortunately, she was the only one who witnessed me making our first batch of cookie dough, the night before our grand opening.

I had nicely whipped the butter and sugar into a beautiful, fluffy batter in our prized twenty-quart Hobart mixer. In went the flour, eggs, vanilla, baking powder, and walnuts. The powerful paddle swirled everything together so nicely that I was somewhat mesmerized as I poured in the chocolate chips from my one-quart glass measuring cup. My hand must have dropped into the bowl as I poured because suddenly the glass was yanked out of my hand by the metal paddle, which continued in its impersonal way to churn the ingredients.

Crunch and crackle replaced the harmonic whoosh that had captivated me.

"Oh God!" I yelled out.

Susan, naturally thinking I had gotten my hand caught in the machine, rushed over. "Are you okay?" she asked, expecting the worst.

"Yeah, but this measuring cup is all ground up in the cookie dough."

As word of my debacle leaked out during opening week I found a way to save a little face with those who wanted to hear the story. After recounting the horror of having the cup ground up in the batter I finished the story by saying, "And it took hours to pick out the glass so we could make these cookies."

This was followed by a silent pause as the listener, entranced by the story as I had been by the Hobart, caught up in one of those nodding, "Yeah, uh huh, oh no," modes as I wove the tale, at last realized he or she had been suckered at the end. I loved the wild-eyed look of horror at the thought of glass-infused cookies followed by the immediate purse-lipped recognition of the scam.

"Gotcha," was my getaway line. It was, however, a meager cover-up for the embarrassment I felt as I witnessed, on an almost daily basis, my kitchen skills betray me.

I think it was the fatigue of long hours and constant pressure that brought about many of these funny and not-so-funny errors. I am pretty sure every restaurant has experienced catastrophes like spilling a five-gallon bucket of pickles on the floor just before the dinner rush, or mixing up the rye flour and white flour, or leaving an empty pot on the stove overnight and finding it in the morning melted to the grill, infusing the atmosphere with unbreathable fumes. We went through a stage when it seemed as if every day brought yet another creative *faux pas*.

I take great solace in legendary stories of kitchen gaffes turning into gastronomic history, such as the origins of crêpes Suzette, which were never supposed to have been set on fire (or so the story goes). The contemporary catch phrase for such turn-arounds is called making lemonade out of lemons. A friend of mine once tried to make chocolate pudding and when the pudding did not set up he served it anyway. He balanced pillows of whipped cream on the liquid chocolate and simply called it Floating Islands, to great acclaim.

One day we mistakenly received an order of fusilli (spiral) pasta instead of our usual flat noodles for the Cajun pasta dish. Instead of sending it back, Susan decided to make pasta salad, a dish we had avoided making because most pasta salads we tasted in restaurants seemed dry and boring. Rising to the challenge, she came up with a great dressing that survived the pasta's ability to absorb. The flavors hold up even after two or three days in the refrigerator. We would simply pull it out two hours before serving to allow the dressing to come to room temperature and coat the noodles. This was one occasion, among many, in which we managed to salvage the lemonade from the lemons. In the restaurant business, we learned, one must become a lemonade maven.

ɞ Pasta Salad

SERVES 4

1 pound dry or fresh fusilli (spiral-shaped) pasta, multi-colored, if available
½ bunch fresh parsley, stemmed and finely chopped
½ basket cherry tomatoes, quartered
One 12-ounce jar roasted red peppers, cut into 1-inch strips
1 small red onion, cut into thin 1-inch long strips

2 tablespoons capers
2 tablespoons caper juice from the jar
½ cup pitted and halved black olives
1 large cucumber, peeled, seeded, and coarsely chopped
Pasta Salad Dressing (recipe follows)
Lettuce leaves to line platter
Freshly grated Parmesan or Romano cheese, to taste
Dried oregano for garnish

Cook the pasta as directed on the package. Rinse with cold water, drain, rinse, drain again, then set aside.

In a mixing bowl combine all the remaining salad ingredients except the dressing, lettuce, cheese, and oregano. Add the cooked pasta and the dressing and toss. Refrigerate for 1 hour to allow the flavors to blend.

To serve, line a platter (or individual plates) with the lettuce. Serve the pasta salad on top of the lettuce, sprinkle on the grated cheese to taste, and then top with a small amount of dried oregano.

❧ Pasta Salad Dressing

ENOUGH FOR 4 SERVINGS OF PASTA SALAD

1 cup extra-virgin olive oil
¼ cup fresh lemon juice
¼ cup fresh lime juice
¼ cup red wine vinegar (good-quality Burgundy, if possible)
5 large cloves garlic, peeled
2 tablespoons capers

2 tablespoons caper juice from the jar
¼ teaspoon whole black peppercorns
Salt, to taste

Combine all the ingredients in a blender and purée until creamy.

More Joys of Fermentation

&· Bread is fermented grain and beer is often called liquid bread. Wine- and cheese-making also require a fermentation process. All of these foods share an attribute: They elicit intense passion among their followers. Many who are fascinated with one tend to love them all. Brine pickling is another type of fermentation process and, in some cultures, is considered as important as bread. Think of Korea without *kim chee* or Germany without sauerkraut? These are two cultures that are practically defined by a common fiber: fermented cabbage!

What I like about *kim chee*, a spicy sauerkraut, is that it combines so many of my personal food passions into one product: cabbage, garlic, hot peppers, fermentation, and tradition.

While living at our retreat center, I used to love making pickled foods in late summer, just after the cabbage and cucumber harvest. We had a small storeroom that held a fairly constant temperature. I kept vats of salt-brined cucumber pickles, *kim chee*, and sauerkraut bubbling away for about four weeks, so that they would be ready just in time for our annual harvest fair where they often won blue ribbons.

Brine pickling, which is the fermenting of vegetables in a salt bath, probably made more sense in the days before refrigeration.

With our contemporary concerns about sodium intake, the pickle is in danger of becoming a vegetable non grata, but anyone who grew up fishing for kosher pickles in a barrel is going to have a hard time giving them up.

Similarly, *kim chee* is an addictive food. It can, quite seriously, light up your mouth; to appreciate it though, you need to like spicy food. If you do not, there is always sauerkraut, which is really the same thing but without the garlic and cayenne. It is hard for me to imagine people in Germany eating large quantities of garlic and cayenne, but as our world shrinks and we head toward a global diet the image of *kim chee* in Bavaria no longer seems so far-fetched.

What You Will Need to Make Pickles, Sauerkraut, and Kim Chee

The procedures for all three are similar. You need a salt brine solution, a fairly constant temperature, and the ingredients for brining. The usual formula is 1 cup of salt for every gallon of water. However, you may cut back to as little as ¾ cup of salt per gallon if you are concerned about salt intake. The flavors will be blander and there is a greater chance of spoilage, but it will be less salty.

To make each of these you will need either a large ceramic crock or a plastic bucket. You will also need a weight that is slightly smaller than the top of your container, such as a plate or a weighted plastic lid. This is to keep everything submerged. The containers and weights need to be sterilized to avoid contamination and off flavors. Simply submerge them in boiling water for 1 minute.

The aging location should be away from sunlight, and with a temperature between 55 and 70 degrees. Warmer temperatures will speed up fermentation but will also cause more mold or off flavors.

ເຂົ Dill Pickles

To avoid having to move the filled container, which leads to spill-age, prepare these in the same location where they will be aged. You will need a moderately cool place, where the temperature will remain constant, near 60 degrees.

Pickling cucumbers (there are many types), picked small or
  medium, not bruised or cut, and weighed
Pickling spice blend (1 tablespoon per pound of cucumbers):
  equal parts whole coriander seed, whole mustard seed, whole
  peppercorns, and whole dill seed
Fresh dill (1 cup, loosely packed, per 20 pounds of
  cucumbers)
Whole fresh cloves garlic (10 cloves per 20 pounds of
  cucumbers)
Whole bay leaves (10 per 20 pounds of cucumbers)
Salt (1 cup per gallon of water)
Water, at room temperature

Wash the cucumbers in cold water. Be careful not to bruise or cut the skins. Remove any dirt or extraneous matter. Fill the container(s) almost full (2 inches from the top) with cucumbers, packing tightly but not forcing.

Add the spice blend, dill, bay leaves, and garlic. The amount depends on the weight of the cucumbers (see ingredients above).

Mix the salt in the water until it dissolves. Cover the cucumbers and spices with the salt solution, filling the tubs until the brine is 2 inches from the top of the container. Put a weight on the cucumbers, submerging them; do not allow any to float to the top. Cover loosely with a lid or cheesecloth (to keep things from falling or flying in). If necessary, top off with more salted water, to a level ½ inch from the top of the container.

Allow the cucumbers to ferment for 2 to 4 weeks. Every day or two check to be sure no pickles are exposed to the air. After a few days a whitish scum will form on the surface. Skim this off and discard; if removed regularly, it will not harm the flavor. Add plain water, if necessary, to replace evaporated brine.

Taste the brine periodically. The saltiness should give way to a sour flavor within 2 to 4 weeks, but it can happen earlier or later depending on the temperature and other conditions. If any pickles are exposed to the air for a few days they may begin to mold or rot. If so, discard the offenders immediately. When the brine begins to taste pickled, try one of the cucumbers. When the flavor is how you like it, jar up the pickles with enough brine to cover them, and refrigerate. These should keep for a few months with only a gradual change: Remember, the brine is still active so there will continue to be slow fermentation, even in the fridge.

N O T E : This technique works with other vegetables as well, such as cauliflower, bell and chile peppers, carrots, onions, and baby corn.

৵ Sauerkraut

4 heads green cabbage, shredded
1 cup salt

1 gallon water
3 tablespoons whole caraway seed (optional)

Because cabbage will release its own juices, you need not cover it with as much water as when making pickles. Dissolve the salt in the water. Add enough water so that the cabbage, when pressed by the weight, is just submerged. During the next few days the liquid content will appear to have increased.

From this point, follow the same procedures for making pickles, allowing about 4 weeks for the kraut to fully ferment (the time may vary depending on the temperature of your room). Remember to skim off any surface scum and make sure the cabbage stays submerged in the brine. When it is pickled to your satisfaction, store the sauerkraut with the brine in covered glass or plastic containers and refrigerate. It will keep for about 3 months. If it begins to overferment, bring it to a boil in a small pot, which will arrest the fermentation. You may then keep it for another month, or longer, in the refrigerator.

♁ Kim Chee

You can make this more or less spicy by adjusting the amounts of chiles and cayenne. Follow instructions for making the sauerkraut but omit the caraway seed and add:

1 tablespoon cayenne
25 cloves fresh garlic, peeled and left whole
10 whole pods dried chile peppers, preferably *arbol* peppers

As with sauerkraut, make sure there is enough liquid to

cover all the ingredients. The garlic cloves will pickle along with the cabbage and are delicious to eat. The hot peppers may be too hot for most people but I have a few friends who eat them along with the cabbage. *Kim chee* takes the same amount of time to ferment as sauerkraut, about 4 weeks, depending on temperature. Store it the same way, refrigerated in covered glass or plastic containers.

GUMBO, CHILI,

&

SOUPS

As the *Roux* Is to Gumbo . . .

❧ The jazz trumpeter Wynton Marsalis and B. B. King were trying to explain the blues to Ted Koppel one late night on TV. B. B. ran out of words and finally had to let Lucille (his guitar) explain it for him. Wynton, however, drew an interesting analogy, saying that blues is the root of all music because it is, "as the *roux* is to the gumbo. It is the foundation, but also the hardest part to make."

I love gumbo. Not just the taste, the whole idea of it. Gumbo is a simple variation of soup or stew, but it has something extra going for it that provides a dimension which satisfies on a deeper level. It has *roux*.

The gumbo we made at Brother Juniper's Café was our own version and it was thick with *roux*. We served the gumbo in a soup bowl but not with rice, as is customary in Louisiana. We presented it as a thick soup and served it with one of our wheat and buttermilk rolls.

Gumbo transcends normal stew because of the *roux*, in which flour and oil are cooked together until the paste (*roux*) darkens to a golden brown. Simple flour is changed into a rich toasty stew base, which is the prerequisite for good gumbo. When it is added to the stew an underlying, deeply enjoyable flavor is captured. Good *roux* requires patience and perseverance because it means staying at the stove for at least forty-five minutes, stirring the pot. If you take your attention from it the *roux* will burn, which means you have to throw it out and start again.

There are degrees of *roux,* from light to dark. Though I prefer the dark in most gumbos, most of our customers preferred a medium *roux,* which was cooked to a caramel color. Dark *roux* looks more like milk chocolate.

One time I made the deepest darkest *roux* imaginable. My intent was to push the envelope to its furthest reaches and I think in the process I fell off the edge of the earth. The normal forty-five minutes had elapsed and I, Mr. Roux, as Susan facetiously called me, stood patiently over my pot, stirring and explaining to anyone who happened to enter the kitchen how amazing this particular batch of gumbo was going to be.

I was preparing a special Mardi Gras meal for our community. The previous year Susan and I, along with a small group of musicians and performers, had staged a night at the "Thibideau Fountaineau Hotel." It was a full-blown production, replete with a cast of stereotypical Cajun characters in a mini-passion play about love in the bayou, climaxed with some great music, including a rousing version of Hank Williams's "Jambalaya." We based our menu on the three dishes in the song: jambalaya, a rice and shrimp casserole; crawfish pie, for which we made crayfish *etouffée* because of Calvin Trillin's passion for it and my passion for Calvin Trillin's food essays; and filé gumbo. This was also the night I invented Cajun Three-Pepper Bread, which is described in *Brother Juniper's Bread Book.* The meal was such a success that I decided to repeat it the following Mardi Gras (1986), even though we did not have the time to put a show together because we were working furiously on the opening of Brother Juniper's Café. What I did want to do was to top the previous year's menu by preparing the greatest gumbo ever made. The key, I reasoned, was my new-found knowledge of *roux,* gleaned from the writings of Paul Prudhomme and Justin Wilson.

There I stood, transfixed by my *roux.* At forty minutes the *roux* had turned a beautiful light caramel, my usual stopping point. But tonight, I decided, it was going to be dark chocolate in color. I continued to stir. At sixty minutes, the *roux* looked like milk chocolate and my friend Sr. Christina, a good arbiter of the community's tolerance for new taste encounters, urged me to pull it from the flame. "No way," I declared. "Tonight we're going for the ultimate gumbo."

At one hour and fifteen minutes, the chocolate color was coming in deeper and deeper and, at last, I was satisfied that the only tone left to achieve would be charcoal. I mixed my ultimate *roux* into the heavenly array of shrimp, clams, sausage, and "holy trinity" vegetables (more on these follow). Then I tasted. My mind and taste buds began a difficult debate. The flavor was so intense that it was not enjoyable. My mind kept rationalizing, saying, "This gumbo is great! Stop being a sissy." The thought of abandoning ten pounds of Aidells andouille sausage (my favorite), ten pounds of succulent jumbo prawns, and ten pounds of juicy chopped clams created a pressure between my eyes that made it extremely difficult to arrive at a clear decision. I was about to serve it, despite my reservations, when Sr. Christina came back into the kitchen and compassionately said, "Brother Peter, I know what you must be going through right now, especially after an hour and fifteen minutes of *roux*-making, but I think if you serve this gumbo it will be a big mistake."

I took her word for it and postponed the meal long enough to put together a fifteen minute *roux,* strain out the sausage, shrimp, and clams, find some more clam broth, and whip together a substitute quickie gumbo that, amazingly, drew oohhs and aahhs from the crowd. I saved a small amount of the earlier "ultimate" gumbo and, as a penance, ate a big bowl later that

night, thinking about my arrogance, boldness, and lack of courage, fighting off the temptation to judge everyone else for scaring
me down to a fifteen-minute *roux*. I was inspired, in this striving,
by the remembrance that the next day was the beginning of Lent
and by the unavoidable admission that the gumbo was, if not
burnt then, at best, over the edge, a Mardi Gras reprobate with
little or no chance of redemption. I have kept my *roux* all under
one hour since then.

The application of heat causes *roux* to change flavors, attaining a
tonal quality impossible to achieve in a basic flour and oil blend.
Many soups and stews are thickened with a simple three-minute
roux, easy to execute and effective as a thickener, but sorely
lacking in character. The beauty of gumbo *roux* is that it adds
another dimension to the stew; it has its own special character
yet it disappears, subordinating its own identity to that of the
sausage, seafood, poultry, or other ingredients. It may take forty-
five minutes to make, but it forms the necessary base upon which
the rest of the gumbo is built. As Wynton says, "*Roux* is the
foundation."

Here are some questions that often arise about gumbo: What is
filé in reference to gumbo? What role does okra play? What is the
"holy trinity" of gumbo? Why is it so spicy?

Filé refers to a powder made from the ground leaves of the
sassafras tree. It both flavors and helps thicken gumbo, but is
used primarily for its flavor, which is similar to that of green tea,
and is delightful but not necessary in all gumbos. Filé is now
available in most supermarkets.

Okra is generally one of the least appreciated vegetables in
America. This is because it is slimy (unless it is batter-fried and
crisped to perfection). In gumbos, okra also acts as a thickening
agent and lends flavor as well. Incidentally, "gumbo" is another

name for okra, which indicates the more prominent role okra played in gumbos in the past, probably before the American sensitivity to slimy things took over. My sister-in-law, Terri Saxon, is very involved in staging a festival in Irmo, South Carolina, called the Okra Strut so, thankfully, okra has not gone out of favor everywhere.

The "holy trinity" refers to the use of bell peppers, onion, and celery, which are found in many Cajun recipes. These are usually diced and sautéed and, like *roux*, are part of the foundation of good Cajun food. Why and how this combination became so prevalent is anyone's guess, but it probably has to do with what grows well in Louisiana. As Cajun and Creole cuisines are the result of cultures that are themselves hybrids of French, African, Nova Scotian, and Spanish, so, too, is the food a blending of diverse ingredients.

Cajun food is legendary for its spiciness and use of chile peppers. One of the big tourist attractions in Louisiana is the Tabasco headquarters on Avery Island, where the McIlhenny family developed a pepper sauce that is one of the most successful products in history. In his book *Paul Prudhomme's Louisiana Kitchen*, Paul Prudhomme says, "There are many results to be had from peppers, and of course 'heat' is one of them. But the ultimate purpose of peppers is to achieve flavors, and these flavors are sensations in the palate that come at different times—when you first put a bite of food in your mouth, when you're chewing it, after you swallow it. Each kind of pepper works differently and when they are balanced correctly they achieve an 'after-you-swallow' glow." I call this the loyalty factor, which means you can eat it now but still taste it hours later.

Gumbo is a uniquely American amalgamation of cultures, ingredients, flavors, and variations. Its success depends upon a simple foundation born out of the hardships of life in the bayou: a dark *roux*, which expresses the highest exaltations of the human spirit. The longer you cook it and the darker you make it, the more intense the gumbo. As Wynton so aptly assessed: The *roux* is to the gumbo as the blues is to music.

🦢 To Make and Use *Roux*

MAKES 2 CUPS

2½ cups flavorless vegetable oil (canola, peanut, or safflower)
1 cup unbleached all-purpose flour

First, make sure you use a heavy-bottomed fry pan or sauce-pan as it needs to conduct heat for a long time without burning the flour and oil. There are varying formulas for the flour/oil ratio, but the simplest to remember and to work with is 2½ parts flour to 1 part oil. Use a vegetable oil with little taste of its own, such as peanut, safflower, or canola (although some cooks have suggested bacon fat—substitute it at your own discretion). Use all-purpose flour, bleached or unbleached. Do not use whole-wheat flour because the bran will burn. Whisk the two ingredients together in the pan until all the flour is incorporated, then cook over medium heat, stirring with a wooden or metal spoon. You can step away for a few seconds at a time but it is safest to keep the mixture moving, stirring and scraping across the entire surface of the pan to avoid any burning. You may see specks of brown developing on the bottom, which is okay. Stir them in. However, if the specks are black, the flame is too high and the *roux* is burning. If it seems to be coloring too quickly or unevenly, turn down the heat. After the first 5 minutes, reduce the heat to medium-low and permit no interruptions.

There are schools of esoteric thought when it comes to the direction and pattern of stirring sauces and gravies. I have heard intricate rationales for clockwise or counter-clockwise spiral patterns (always from the outside to the center) and, believe me, I have tried them all. The value of a pattern is its thoroughness and meditative attributes. On the other hand, there is always a danger of going to "automatic pilot" in which you become so entranced and fixed in your pattern that thinking ceases and the ability to respond diminishes. For instance, if the phone rings you have to be present enough to remember to turn off the heat. You can always come back to a partially finished *roux* at any time. If you do need to turn off the heat, remember to keep stirring for a while as the pan is still red hot. And take the pan off an electric range as it takes a while for the coil to cool down. These are just little examples of the importance of alertness. There are great misconceptions about meditations on food but, traditionally, the value of true meditation is too increase awareness of the moment, not to space out. *Roux* will keep you mindful of this necessity.

At different stages of the process, the *roux* will change color, going from pasty white, to light caramel, to golden brown, to milk chocolate, and eventually to dark chocolate in hue.

If you decide to use a very dark *roux,* taste it first and make sure it does not taste burned; the flavor of the *roux* will affect the entire gumbo. If you do discern any burnt flavor, throw it out and begin again.

When the *roux* is almost the color you want, remove the pan from the heat. It will continue to darken for a few more minutes because it is extremely hot. Transfer the *roux* to a metal bowl to protect it from burning, or continue stirring for another 3 minutes.

To add *roux* to gumbo, the trick is to do it without getting lumps. Here are a few general tips:

· Reserve a few cups of cooled soup liquid, while simultaneously bringing the rest of the soup to a simmer. In a blender or with a whisk, mix the *roux* with the cool liquid until smooth (if you try to do this with hot liquid it will immediately thicken into an unworkable glop). Then, gradually whisk the *roux*/liquid mixture into the simmering soup.

· The thickening ability of *roux* diminishes the longer and darker you make it so be sure to have enough on hand.

· Save any leftover *roux* for another day. So make a fair amount of it to have on hand. Keep it refrigerated; it should be fine for at least 2 weeks. Eventually it may turn moldy, so do not plan to keep it indefinitely.

· Cooled *roux* is easy to blend into cooled soup stock as there is no heat to make it lump up. If using hot *roux*, refer to the first tip above.

· Another option is to make the *roux* in a heavy-bottomed soup pot, then add the hot soup stock, from another pot, directly to it, whisking quickly to avoid the formation of lumps. The important point is to thicken it quickly. Do not add *roux* to a pot full of cold stock and then try to bring the whole thing to a boil. This usually causes sticking and burning, because the *roux* tends to sink to the bottom of the pot. Regardless of the method, the key is a smooth blending of *roux* and soup, the result of which is memorable gumbo.

ࠖ Filé Gumbo

SERVES 8

This is our own version of gumbo, so do not expect it to conform to any preconceptions based on your visits to restaurants such as

Commander's Palace, Brennan's, K-Paul's, or Chez Helene. It makes use of my favorite ingredients: clams, shrimp, and sausage. As with many recipes of traditional dishes, you must feel empowered to branch off into your own variations. You may prefer to add chicken, oysters, mussels, and yes, even okra. After following the recipe as written you should, if the gumbo touches you the way it does me, be inspired by your own ideas. Perhaps we should call this Brother Juniper's Law: A good recipe unlocks creativity to inspire an even better one.

Spice Blend
1 teaspoon coarsely ground black pepper
1 tablespoon filé powder
3 tablespoons Tabasco or Brother Juniper's Chile Peppermash
   (page 6)
1 teaspoon dried oregano
3 whole bay leaves
½ cup chopped fresh parsley

2 large cans (46 ounces each) clam or chicken broth, or a
   combination of the two
6 tablespoons peanut, vegetable, or olive oil
2 cups diced onion
1 cup diced green bell pepper (For a spicier gumbo, use fresh
   chiles, such as Anaheim and Fresno (both medium-hot), or
   serrano and jalapeño (both hot), instead of the mild bell.)
1 cup diced red pepper (hot or mild)
1 cup diced celery
10 cloves garlic, peeled and finely chopped
1½ pounds andouille or Creole sausage (you can substitute
   other smoked sausage, such as kielbasa or linguica, if
   necessary), sliced into rounds, ¼ inch thick
1 pound large shrimp, peeled and deveined

2 cups medium or dark *roux* (I suggest "milk chocolate" colored.)
1½ pounds chopped or baby clams with juice
4 tablespoons white vinegar
2 tablespoons tamari (soy sauce)

Make spice blend: In a bowl combine all the ingredients. Set aside.

Reserve 3 cups of the clam or chicken broth. In a heavy-bottomed soup pot bring the remaining broth to a boil and let it simmer. Meanwhile, in a skillet sauté the onions, all the peppers, and celery in 4 tablespoons of the oil for about 5 minutes, or until they begin to sweat and turn bright. Add the garlic, stir 1 minute, and remove the pan from the heat. Stir in the spice blend and transfer the mixture from the skillet to a bowl.

Sauté the sausage and shrimp in the 2 remaining table-spoons oil until the shrimp turn pink, about 5 minutes. Transfer to the bowl of vegetables and spices.

Add the *roux* to the simmering stock by first whisking or blending the 3 cups of reserved broth (not heated) with the *roux* to thin it. Quickly whisk the thinned *roux* into the simmering stock. It should dissolve and immediately thicken the broth. Add the clams and stir for 1 minute over medium-low heat; maintain a simmer. Add all the vegetable/spice/shrimp/sausage mixture, the vinegar, and tamari, and continue to stir until the gumbo returns to a simmer. Remove the pan from the heat. If the gumbo is not spicy enough, add more Tabasco or peppermash.

The gumbo can be served over rice, as a soup with a roll, or with corn bread on the side. A few sprigs of fresh parsley on top make a nice, simple garnish.

Chili Does Not Belong to

Texas Only

*To enjoy chili, we need only spoon it up and fire the mouth
with its powerful pungency. But to touch the passion that
men feel for it, we have to do more than taste it, we have to
stare deep into its restless, lonely heart.*
—John Thorne, *Just Another Bowl of Texas Red*

One person's chili is another's beef stew.
—Peter Reinhart, *Brother Juniper's Bread Book*

&❧ The first thing one discovers when entering the serious chili
world is the narrow definition of what constitutes true chili—
specifically, Texas chili. Cincinnati chili is scoffed at, while Carib-
bean-style chili is not even considered chili. Anyone entering an
innovative variation of the classic "Big Red" in a chili contest
does so knowing that most of the judges probably will not even
taste it, wanting to protect their taste buds from contamination
by unorthodox seasonings. Never have I seen such strict devotion, except in a few spiritual communities. *Chili heads*, as they
are known among themselves, are just as dogmatic about their
convictions as newly converted Christians.

Competition Texas chili is not usually found at most restaurants because of the time and expense required in making it.

While commercial chili is chock full of beans, which makes it a very economical food, there are no beans of any kind to be found in pure Texas chili. Beans are considered filler. The competition ethic goes back to the days of chuck wagons and cattle ranges. The mettle of a range cook was determined, to a great degree, by his chili.

Chili meant meat and sauce, nothing else. Southwest spices such as dried peppers, cumin, and oregano seasoned the sauce. Despite the simplicity of the concept there are, as thousands of chili cook-offs have proven, an infinite number of ways to make Texas chili. A good chili cook can capture countless flavor shadings, aromas, and variations in texture.

This may be heretical, and will probably cost me my membership in the ICS (International Chili Society), but there are also plenty of ways to make great chili that do not conform to the stringent rules of cook-offs. Many regions of the country, and indeed the world, have their own variations, all just as delicious as the Texas-style. The debate is akin to the unresolved barbecue disputes. Is it possible to compare North Carolina pepper/vinegar pork barbecue to South Carolina mustard-based pork to Texas beef brisket or to Memphis or St. Louis ribs in red sauce? Is it fair to compare Texas chili, with its rigid parameters, to Cincinnati chili, with its innovative cinnamon spicing? Though it is reasonable to prefer one to another, let's end the regional biases. Almost any kind of chili is better than no chili.

There were two types of chili lovers at Brother Juniper's Café: regular (with meat) and black bean (vegetarian, which is discussed in another chapter). We honored all chili traditions, but bent the knee to none. Ours was as original as everything else we made, neotraditional rather than Texas classic. It was an everyday version of "Big Red," but with a few unique twists and turns to set it apart. We also, to the horror of the purists, proudly (and economically) used kidney beans.

One of our regular customers was a kid of about fourteen, a large boy who wrestled and played on his school's football team. He was hooked on our chili. He usually came in with his mother, who was there simply to buy a loaf of bread. Each time they came in he pleaded with her for a cup of chili until she relented. Later, when he was about sixteen, he regularly dropped by on his own to buy a bowl and a refill. He referred to it as "outrageous chili," or, simply, "killer." Through his and a few others' efforts, the chili became "legendary," at least locally. Later, when he turned nineteen, the boy came to work for us in the bakery. Three years after we closed the restaurant, he still spoke in awed terms about the chili and his memories of it. The newer employees, their experience of chili limited to the stuff that comes in cans, could never quite fathom the hold this chili had on him. He had become, to their bewilderment, a "chili head."

I have often wondered what it is about chili that makes it so special to so many. There have been many books and essays addressing the subject of chili passion. I once saw in an old book a blessing for chili in which a cowboy thanked God for granting him something that not even the Chinese have. It is possible, I suppose, to develop a theory based on nostalgia, the wistful longing for simpler days on the range, but I do not think this gets to the heart of the matter.

There are many factors that have elevated chili to the status of, quite possibly, the truly definitive national dish of the United States (and there is currently a movement afoot to have it so declared). The use of chile peppers as a central spice predates the arrival of the explorer/invaders from Western Europe. Judeo-Christian cultures have a great ability to adopt, adapt, and subsume native cultures. Just as the Romans "baptized" the pre-Christian rituals and festivals of the Druids, so too has chili moved from the roots into the leaves of western culture. In the Southwest United States, as well as in Central and South

America, the ingredients of chili are a component of our human clay in the same way that our blood chemistry is so much like the sea's, causing certain ocean broths to go down as easily as mother's milk. Indigenous foods resonate with people raised on the same soil, even if we are, like most Americans, nothing more than transplants, indigenous wanna-bes.

From what I have seen at chili cook-offs, the flavors and spices of chili have a strong, intoxicating hold on the psyches of the participants, like soma in Huxley's *Brave New World*. Chili causes some people to act, well, irrationally (there, I've said it). Primal reversion, vicarious cowboy syndrome, call it what you will, there is a love-fest spirit at chili cook-offs. Chili, at events like this, reveals itself to be a powerful symbol of a country in search of itself, paying tribute to itself, and, in a subtle, probably subconscious manner, honoring the root stock upon which it has grafted itself. Now, if we could only get the judges to loosen up a little and realize that chili does not belong to Texas only . . .

ࣦ Neo-Texas Chili

SERVES 6

2 pounds cooked beef brisket, plus all pan juice (You may
   substitute 2 pounds cooked ground beef, drained of all
   grease, but this will not be as good as the brisket.)
2 cups uncooked dried kidney beans
10 cups water (5 cups for soaking the beans; 5 cups for
   cooking them)
   Chili Powder
4 tablespoons paprika

1 tablespoon cayenne
1 tablespoon salt
½ tablespoon dried oregano

1 tablespoon vegetarian beef-flavored soup base (page 110; add
    if using ground beef instead of brisket, to replace brisket pan
    juices)
1 tablespoon vegetable or olive oil
2 cups diced onions
1 cup diced mild or hot chile peppers, or a mixture of both
6 large cloves fresh garlic, minced
1½ cups diced fresh tomatoes, or one 14-ounce can crushed
    tomatoes with juice
1 tablespoon Brother Juniper's Chile Peppermash (page 6) or
    Tabasco
½ teaspoon freshly ground black pepper
Salt to taste
    Garnishes
Susan's Spicy Red and Green Salsas (pages 8 and 9)
diced onion
grated Cheddar or jack cheese
sour cream
chopped fresh cilantro

Prepare the meat: If using brisket, follow the directions on
page 140 for Beef Brisket. If you are using ground beef, which
will not be as unique as the brisket, cook it slowly in a large pan
till brown.

Cool the cooked brisket, trim off the fat, and chop the meat
into small pieces, saving the juice. If using ground beef, pour off
the grease and discard. Set the beef aside.

Wash the beans, checking for stones that sometimes are
mixed in with dry beans. Soak the beans in 5 cups water to cover

for at least 4 hours, or overnight. Drain the beans. In a heavy-bottomed pot combine the beans in the 5 cups fresh water. Cover, bring to a boil, and simmer for approximately 1½ hours, or until the beans are soft and begin to split open (some beans may cook in less time). Remove the lid and allow the liquid to cook down until it begins to thicken.

While the beans are cooking, make homemade chili powder: In a bowl combine all the ingredients. (This can be made in larger portions. If so, store what is left over in an airtight jar; it will keep for months.)

Heat the oil in a large skillet and sauté the onions, chiles, and garlic over high heat, stirrring, for 3 minutes. Turn the heat down to medium-low, cover, and continue to cook for an additional 8 minutes, or until the onions are translucent and very soft. Stir in the chili powder, then the chopped meat and brisket pan juices (beef base or boullion cubes, if using ground beef), and cook until hot. Remove from heat.

Add the meat mixture to the undrained beans (in the bean pot), then add the tomatoes, peppermash, and black pepper. Bring to a boil and simmer over medium-low heat until thick, stirring occasionally to prevent sticking, but not too often. (That is called "bothering the pot.")

Add salt to taste, if necessary, remembering that the beans will absorb a lot. Fifteen minutes later, taste and adjust the flavoring. If you prefer a spicier chili, add either more chili powder (mix it into a paste with a little water before adding to the pot) or a hot sauce such as Tabasco.

Have some or all of the following garnishes ready in bowls for serving: Susan's Spicy Red and Green Salsas (pages 8 and 9), diced onion, grated Cheddar or jack cheese, sour cream, and chopped fresh cilantro. Serve the chili in large soup bowls. Sprinkle cheese and onion over the top, put a small dollop of sour cream in the center of each bowl, and top with cilantro. Serve the salsas on the side.

NOTE: Chili always tastes better the next day, after the seasonings have blended. For this reason, when possible, it is a good idea to make it ahead of time. When reheating it, you may need to add a little water as the beans will absorb the juices while cooling.

The Zen of Black Bean Chili

San Francisco is universally regarded as one of the restaurant capitals of the world. On any given night, if everyone who lived in San Francisco decided to go out to eat, there would be enough seats in all the restaurants to accommodate the entire lot. This is an established fact. Not all of these places are world class nor do they all possess the elements of magic, but there are tens of thousands of people who go out every day or night in search of a satisfying meal.

Occasionally a new establishment emerges from the crowd and attracts its fifteen minutes of fame. Sometimes one manages to retain its reputation and existence for many years. In a city where three restaurants go out of business daily (while at least three more debut), this is no simple accomplishment. Aspirations vary, naturally, but within every proprietor there is, I believe, a subconscious urge to nourish, to mother, and to feed the souls of his or her patrons.

There are also those few restaurateurs who have a vision that encompasses the pursuit of festivity, mystery, and magic to which I allude throughout this book. Their expressions of this vision may take on different words, symbols, menus, and business plans but, if boiled down to essences, there is usually an attempt to make contact with the innermost being of everyone who enters their door.

One such restaurant whose vision has inspired me is called Greens, founded by the Zen Center of San Francisco, which has had stunning success because of its creative connection to authentic tradition. The transmission of this connectedness is what empowers their food. What seems to empower their transmission is that they have not forgotten that going out to eat should be a celebration of life—it should be fun. Though the roots of Greens are in the Zen Buddhist tradition, I have always felt that Brother Juniper's and Greens grew from a common well of understanding.

As I understand the idea of zen, it refers to being present in the moment. Some call it "presence." The exercises associated with Zen Buddhism, such as zazen sitting, or contemplating answerless riddles called koans, are all designed to bring the mind into the present, fully focused on the here and now. In the Christian tradition a similar idea is called "bringing the mind into the heart." Personal spiritual powers, however, are pointless unless they bear fruit, usually through service. I think the vision Brother Juniper's shares with Greens is that service can be expressed through feeding people in a daily yet celebratory manner.

At Greens, one is always aware of its Buddhist origins yet never made to feel invaded by foreignness. The food is vegetarian yet does not demand ideological commitment from its patrons. The servers and chefs are often students and priests. Everything works against preconceptions, which is part of the formula. This counterpoint establishes an atmosphere in which the possibility of magic always seems near, as near as the famous Tassajara bread that is a signature of Greens.

It was there, in 1979, that I had my first taste of black bean chili. Inspired and excited, I immediately went home and made my own version, which, seven years later, became one of the most popular dishes at Brother Juniper's Café. Black bean chili, along with our Neo-Texas chili, allowed me to indulge my passion for chiles (peppers) and chilis (stews made from chiles), and to participate vicariously in indigenous Native American culture. Working with chiles is one of the most enjoyable exercises in cooking.

Black bean chili now has a strong symbolic place in my life because of the confluence of Zen Buddhist, Native American, and Christian influences. It will always be a reminder to me of the interconnectedness and commonality that exists between traditions: of the common goal, practice, and method; the distinct yet similar mythology; and the central role of food in bridging realities. If I have a sense of mission about anything, it is to this sense of connecting. In the zen of black bean chili there is one message: there are two worlds, this and the other, which coexist in the present moment, and only in the present moment do they exist at all.

❧ Black Bean Chili

SERVES 8

4 cups uncooked dried black beans

22 cups water (10 cups for soaking the beans; 12 cups for cooking them)

1 tablespoon whole cumin seeds

2 tablespoons vegetable or olive oil

2 medium onions, diced

2 cups diced mild and hot green chile peppers (these will determine the spiciness of your chili, so mix accordingly)

8 large cloves fresh garlic, pressed or minced
3 cups diced fresh tomatoes (about 1¾ pounds), or
   one 28-ounce can crushed tomatoes with juice
1 teaspoon freshly ground black pepper
1 tablespoon salt
2 tablespoons vegetarian beef-flavored soup base (page 110)
4 tablespoons tamari (soy sauce)
   Garnishes
sour cream, yogurt, or *crème fraîche*
chopped fresh cilantro
Susan's Spicy Red and Green Salsas (pages 8 and 9)

Wash the beans, checking for stones by sifting through them (or pour them, a little at a time, on the table and pick through them). Rinse two or three times until the water is clear. Soak the beans at room temperature in the 10 cups water for a minimum of 4 hours, or overnight.

Drain the beans. In a heavy-bottomed pot bring the 12 cups fresh water and the beans to a boil. Reduce to a simmer, (avoid aluminum pots because of reaction with tomatoes), cover, and cook, stirring occasionally, for about 1½ hours, or until the beans soften and the broth begins to thicken. (If using a pressure cooker, follow the procedures from the pressure cooker manual.) Cooking time may vary depending on the size of the beans.

While the beans are cooking, toast the cumin seeds in a dry frying pan by stirring them over medium heat for about 1 minute, or until the seeds begin to crackle and pop. Remove from the pan.

Increase heat to high and pour the oil into the pan. When hot, add the onions, chiles, and garlic and sauté for about 3 minutes, or until the onions begin to turn translucent. Stir in the cumin seeds and immediately turn off the heat. Cover the pan to let everything steam together. Set aside.

When the beans are soft, stir in the onions, peppers, cumin mixture. Add the tomatoes and black pepper. Stir in the salt, soup base, and tamari. The beans will absorb the salty flavor, so check again after 15 minutes to see if more is needed. (I usually add more soy sauce rather than salt.) Simmer the chili until the liquid is reduced and the consistency is between gravy and soup.

Ladle the chili into soup bowls and top with a dollop of sour cream, yogurt, or *crème fraîche*. Garnish with chopped fresh cilantro and a few tablespoons of either Susan's Red or Green Salsa (pages 8 and 9). Have a bowl of extra salsa standing by for those who like to jazz it up.

Digging Horseneck Clams

in Bodega Bay

&. There is no doubt that clam chowder is my favorite soup. I love it in any of its incarnations: Manhattan, New England, or California (my invention, see recipe). On the other hand, like any "favorite" food there is plenty of room for disappointment when certain minimum standards are not met. Just as a poorly made Caesar salad can be a huge letdown, mediocre clam chowder is terribly depressing, especially since making excellent clam chowder is not that difficult.

For years, I have pursued seemingly pointless missions such as the quest for better and better barbecue, or the search for the world's best clam chowder. The game is to find the best version "out there" and attempt to top it. Everyone needs models of excellence, even if imaginary. My clam chowder model exists only in my imagination because I have never had one that made me exclaim, "It doesn't get any better than this!" Granted, my range of experience is limited, and I know there are hundreds, maybe thousands, of people who believe they have either made or tasted the ultimate clam chowder somewhere. My unquenched palate impels me to experiment, to push the limits. At times, I have exceeded the bounds of good taste, the details of which shall remain a private embarrassment, attempting to prepare a truly satisfying bowl of clam chowder. During a five-year period, however, I arrived at three distinctly different versions that each share one common trait: enough clams to sate that little clam "Pac Man" who dwells in the appetite section of our psyche.

A recurrent nightmare of mine is that someone has invented a Ritz Cracker version of clam chowder. Remember the Ritz Cracker apple pie? No apples, just a filling made with pie-flavored cracker pieces. While others anguish over world affairs and conspiracy theories, I worry that someone is getting rich foisting fake clam chowder on the gullible consumer by soaking crackers, or even textured soy granules, in clam juice and then disguising them in a creamy broth and calling it "Ocean-Deep Award-Winning Clam Chowder." There are some commercial chowders that, I am certain, substitute pieces of cardboard for the clams. Enough about my nightmares.

On the Sonoma coast there is a small fishing port called Bodega Bay, near the town of Bodega, where Alfred Hitchcock filmed *The Birds*. But the reason I go there is to dig for horseneck clams during low tide. There are many such hunting places up and down the coast, some more legendary than others, such as Pismo Beach, home of the elusive and delicious Pismo clam. Some beaches feature even more spectacular bivalves, such as two-pound razor clams or the huge Northwest "gooey ducks" (actually spelled *geoducks*, but impossible to pronounce phonetically). Bodega Bay, though, is the closest to where I live and horseneck clams, weighing about a pound each, have a certain attainability about them that is encouraging for novice clam hunters. There is something satisfying about bagging your limit of ten, and it is a realistic number, even for first-timers.

The trick is to look for little sprays of water shooting out of the sand. The horseneck clam has a retractable valve (hence, horseneck) that comes almost to the surface and seems to spit clam cider. Once spotted, you have to dig down ferociously into the sand, following the slithering valve about three feet, to the clam itself. Smart clammers take along a piece of metal or plastic ducting to keep the sand from collapsing the hole. Once found, the clam is easy to extract from its sandy bed and, plop, it lands right in your bucket. They are not anything like East Coast quahogs or even the more standard manilla clams. They are oversized, ugly-looking blobs, too big to fit inside their own shells, hanging out like *Star Wars*'s Jabba the Hutt. The most edible part is the horseneck's valve, which is sliced into steaks and fried like calamari or abalone, or diced for chowder. The body, or belly, is very soft, very clammy, and full of sand. I think it might taste like an oyster if there were incentive to purge the sand. As I have never found anyone else to brave the belly with, my interest inevitably drifted back to the valve.

Hunting horseneck clams in Bodega Bay is, along with foraging mussels off seaside rocks, probably the only hunting I do. I have fished a few times, even caught some barracuda and a hammerhead shark in the Caribbean years ago, and gone crabbing with chicken necks once, but I do not have a taste for it, a passion for the hunt. Harvesting mollusks is about my speed, and all the while I think about new ways to capture the ocean essence in a soup, stew, or chowder. The memories of Bodega Bay that I take into my later years will be of salty wind, the spit of clam cider, nicked hands, fingernails full of wet beach, and footprints that lead to deep holes where oversized clam bellies lay helpless, betrayed by a wandering, snakelike valve. A craving for the sea, to be permeated by the ocean, always accompanies the image.

Making Clam Chowders

One thing I have learned about cooking clams is that they are soft at first, toughen after about 3 minutes in the soup, and stay tough for about 30 minutes. Then they relax and become tender again. Consequently, it is a good idea to make clam soup in advance. Like many things, it will taste better the next day when the flavors have had time to blend.

Here are the two key principles: lots of clams and lots of clam broth. Beyond that, it is merely fine-tuning.

〄 New England Clam Chowder

SERVES 8

This is the classic version, rich, hearty, and definitely not a low-fat soup. You may lower the fat content by omitting the butter and substituting low-fat milk for the whole milk and the half-and-half. You may also leave out the bacon, but that will greatly alter the taste.

1 quart clam juice
2½ pounds chopped clams (fresh or frozen)
2 potatoes, unpeeled, cut into ¼-inch cubes
½ pound uncooked bacon, chopped into small pieces
4 tablespoons butter
2 onions, diced
½ tablespoon dried tarragon
1 teaspoon freshly ground black pepper
8 cloves fresh garlic, minced

2 cups half-and-half
1½ quarts whole milk
1 cup all-purpose flour
1 tablespoon salt, or to taste

Bring the clam juice and clams to a boil in a large soup pot. Reduce to a simmer, add the potatoes, cover, and cook for 30 minutes.

In a large skillet fry the bacon pieces until they begin to crisp and turn golden brown. Remove the pieces to a paper towel to drain, leaving the fat in the pan.

Add the butter to the bacon fat and melt it over medium-high heat. Add the onions and sauté them until translucent. Add the tarragon, black pepper, and garlic, stirring for 1 minute to blend. Put a lid on the pan and turn off the heat; allow the mixture to steam for 5 minutes.

When the clam broth is ready (the potatoes should be soft enough to eat and the clams should be tender), add the onion-herb mixture, bacon, all of the half-and-half plus 1 quart of the milk. Reserve the remaining milk (1 pint) for the next step. Stir frequently to prevent scorching, and bring the liquid to a slow boil.

In a blender or with a whisk, blend the remaining milk with the flour into a paste (*roux*). When the soup comes to a boil, quickly whisk in the flour/milk *roux*. The soup will thicken quickly. When it does, turn off the heat, and add salt to taste. (The amount you need will vary according to the saltiness of the clam juice and bacon.)

To serve, ladle the chowder into soup bowls. A sprinkling of chopped fresh parsley or tarragon, or a dash of paprika make an attractive garnish. Serve with hot French or sourdough bread.

Some people like oyster or saltine crackers, too, so have some handy.

૨૯ California Clam Chowder

SERVES 6

A Brother Juniper's original. Beautiful and colorful, this chowder has no meat or added fat! It is also very easy to make, coming together quickly and easily once everything is assembled.

3 cups chicken broth
1 quart clam juice
1½ pounds chopped clams (fresh or frozen)
1 teaspoon freshly ground black pepper
½ cup cornstarch
½ pound mushrooms, thinly sliced
2 large sweet red bell peppers, seeded and diced
1 bunch scallions (green onions), sliced into ¼-inch pieces
5 teaspoons tamari (soy sauce)
Fresh parsley sprigs for garnish

In a soup pot, bring all the chicken broth and 3 cups of the clam juice to a boil. Add the clams and black pepper and simmer for 30 minutes, or until the clams are tender.

In a small bowl, whisk the cornstarch into the remaining 1 cup clam juice until the cornstarch is dissolved.

When the clams are tender, whisk the cornstarch mixture into the simmering soup. It should thicken quickly, turning cloudy at first, then becoming clear.

Stir in the mushrooms, red peppers, scallions, and tamari.

Bring the soup back to a boil and stir over medium heat for 1 additional minute. Remove the pot from the heat, cover, and let stand for 5 minutes.

To serve, pour the chowder into large soup bowls and garnish each with a sprig of fresh parsley.

❧ Sweet Red Pepper Clam Chowder

SERVES 6

This soup is an alternative to Manhattan clam chowder, which is a tomato-based soup. In this version, sweet red peppers or pimientos replace the tomatoes as the base, making a beautiful as well as delicious presentation. I think of this as a September soup, when the harvest is in its final explosion and the peppers have changed from immature green to a sweet and voluptuous red.

4 cups clam juice
2 medium potatoes, unpeeled, diced
1 pound chopped or baby clams with juice
2 tablespoons olive oil
1 medium onion, diced
6 large cloves fresh garlic, minced
6 large sweet red bell peppers or pimientos, seeded and diced
½ teaspoon dried marjoram
½ teaspoon freshly ground black pepper
½ cup dry or semi-dry white wine
1 teaspoon salt
4 tablespoons minced fresh basil for garnish

In a soup pot, bring the clam juice and potatoes to a boil and simmer for 20 minutes. Remove the potatoes to a bowl with a slotted spoon or strainer and set them aside. Add the clams to the pot and simmer them for at least 20 minutes.

In a skillet or frying pan, heat the olive oil over high heat. Sauté the onion and garlic until the onion is soft. Add the red peppers and cook until they are bright red and shiny, about 3 minutes. Add the marjoram and black pepper, stir until mixed, and remove from heat.

In a blender or food processor, purée the onion/pepper mixture with the potatoes.

Whisk the purée mixture into the clam juice. Bring the soup back to a boil, add the wine and salt, and remove the pot from the heat.

Serve immediately in soup bowls or a tureen, sprinkling fresh basil over the top. The basil not only garnishes but counterpoints the sweet pepper flavor.

Various Penicillins

ᔥ Many people came into Brother Juniper's Café because of the soups. It was not simply because they wanted soup but more because they wanted what soup represents: nurturing. Susan was the chief soup maker during the first two years and her soups established her as the Molly Goldberg of Forestville. (Does anybody even remember Molly Goldberg, the archetypal Jewish Mother of 1950s television?) During rainy season, when flu and common colds were rampaging, folks would come in with empty gallon jugs to be filled with chicken soup or whatever daily penicillin was on the stove. Sometimes Susan would send a jug of soup home with someone on the intuition that his or her spouse or children might need it. I think this was probably the most rewarding aspect of the business for Susan, when she could conduct ministry on her terms, in her way. These were the times we could look at each other, through bloodshot, barely-opened eyes and say, "See, it is worth it."

We also learned quite a bit about soup making. While I have a tendency toward *roux*-thickened soups, Susan is partial to reduction or purée-thickening. This, naturally, is a more flavorful approach (except in the case of gumbo, which requires dark *roux*). It also requires more time and a good touch with seasonings.

Many of these soups can be made into variations. For instance, chicken tortellini is just a variation of chicken noodle, or chicken rice, or chicken and dumplings. In the following recipes I will leave these variations to your imagination and simply lay down the fundamental "mother" soups.

Soup stocks are fun to work with and I always advocate them, especially as an ecological act of recycling. However, this is not always convenient for home cooks so it is important not to be ashamed to resort to canned broths and powder or paste seasoning blends. These can often add just the touch of richness or flavor needed to put the soup over the top. The main caution is to beware of oversalting when using these concentrated seasonings as they are full of salt. We have discovered a number of natural soup bases that do not use MSG. These can usually be found at natural food markets. They are vegetarian in nature, but can be made to taste like meat or chicken.

I call our soups penicillins in tribute to all the myths surrounding chicken soup. They are myths not because I disbelieve them but, on the contrary, because myths are symbol stories of truth. Soups, and not just chicken soup, emerge from the cauldrons of the hearth, the realm of the all-encompassing Mother. They do not simply heal; they represent healing. Conscientious soup making is an act of participation in the myth of the nurturing God. The following soups are our contribution to the ever-unfolding outreach of this reality.

INGREDIENT NOTE: Some of the soups that follow call for the addition of "soup base." This is a vegetable protein or yeast product (depending upon the brand) found in most natural food stores. It can be made to simulate either chicken or beef flavors. Experiment with them until you find the brand and flavors you prefer. In the recipes below, I will simply refer to "soup base" and you may use your brand of choice (which means you may have to adjust amounts according to the strength of your base). You may also substitute tamari (a strong soy sauce) for the soup base, if you prefer.

IMPORTANT HINT: There is an invaluable tool available at most kitchen or housewares stores called a gravy separator. One brand is called a "souper skimmer." It consists of a plastic measuring cup (we use a 4-cupper, though smaller ones are available) with a long spout that connects to the bottom of the cup. When you fill it with hot soup stock, the fat floats to the top. By slowly pouring the stock through the spout you transfer it out, leaving only the fat in the cup. You can then discard the fat. This is the best way to degrease hot stock. An alternative is to cool it for a few hours in the refrigerator and wait until the fat hardens. Then, remove it. A "souper skimmer" will allow you to finish making your soups without the cooling process.

੩ Susan's Chicken Soup

SERVES 8

18 cups water
1 whole chicken, giblets and neck kept separate
8 whole cloves garlic plus 18 cloves, minced
12 whole peppercorns
1 onion, quartered, *plus* 2 onions, coarsely chopped
1 carrot, sliced into ¼-inch-thick half-moons
2 stalks celery, sliced into ¼-inch-thick pieces
2 tablespoons very finely minced fresh ginger
2 teaspoons freshly ground black pepper
¼ cup vegetarian chicken-flavored soup base (page 110)
¼ cup tamari (soy sauce)

1½ teaspoons salt
½ bunch fresh parsley, chopped

In a small saucepan, bring 2 cups of the water to a boil.
Add the chicken giblets and neck. Cover and simmer for 1 hour.
Strain and save the giblet broth. Discard the neck and giblets (or
give the giblets to your pet for a tasty treat).

Simultaneously, rinse the chicken off under cold water, then
put it in a large soup pot along with the 8 whole cloves garlic, the
quartered onion, and peppercorns. Cover with the remaining 16
cups water. Bring the water to a boil. Simmer, uncovered, for a
minimum of 2 hours, but preferably overnight (use #2 setting if
using an electric stove, or a low flame if using gas). The liquid
should reduce by about 25 percent. Remove the pot from the
heat and let the stock cool for 1 hour before handling.

Pour the stock through a strainer or colander, separating it
from all chicken meat, skin, bones, peppercorns, onions, and
garlic. Set the meat aside to cool. Remove the chicken fat from
the stock by either cooling it (in the refrigerator) until the fat
hardens (this will take a few hours), or using a gravy separator or
"souper skimmer" (page 111). Discard the chicken fat and pour
the stock back in the pot. Continue skimming until all fat is
removed.

Pick through the chicken, discarding all skin, bones, garlic,
peppercorns, and onion. Save the meat, chop it coarsely, and put
it in the stock.

Add the carrot, remaining chopped onions, minced garlic,
celery, ginger, and pepper to the pot. Also add the giblet broth.
Then, add the soup base, tamari, and salt. Bring the soup to a
boil and simmer, uncovered, for 1 hour, reducing the stock.

Taste and adjust the seasonings. Five minutes before serving, add the chopped parsley.

❧ HOW TO MAKE GREAT CHICKEN STOCK

It is always helpful to have chicken stock on hand since it forms the base of so many soups. While commercially made, canned broth is perfectly acceptable, here is a simple way to make exceptional chicken stock, better than anything you can buy in the store:

· Whenever you roast chicken (or turkey), or, if you bone uncooked chicken, save the carcasses. Put them in a roasting pan and place in a preheated 400 degree oven for approximately 35 to 40 minutes, until they turn a beautiful mahogany gold.

· Put the roasted carcasses in a pot of water (8 cups for each carcass), bring to a boil, and simmer, uncovered, until the liquid is reduced by half. This should take 1 to 3 hours, depending on how much you are boiling. The stock will thicken as it reduces. Season with salt and pepper to taste.

· Let the stock cool, strain out the carcasses, and skim off the fat. The resulting stock will keep for up to 6 months in the freezer.

VARIATIONS: chicken tortellini, chicken noodle, and chicken rice. Simply add already cooked pasta or rice to the soup. If you use uncooked pasta or rice, it will absorb a good amount of broth, thickening the soup, necessitating additional liquid and seasoning adjustments.

NOTE FROM SUSAN: During winter months, especially cold and flu season, double the amount of garlic and ginger.

ど French Onion Soup

SERVES 8

This recipe calls for beef bones, but a perfectly respectable stock can be made with vegetarian beef-flavored soup base. We had so many requests from vegetarians for this soup that we made it without real meat. However, the following recipe is the original version and is richer than the vegetarian one. Either way, the real trick in this soup is to caramelize lots of onions.

5 pounds beef soup bones
8 cups water
¼ pound unsalted butter
1 tablespoon vegetable oil
1 tablespoon olive oil
3 pounds white or yellow onions, sliced into half-moon strips
   (use Vidalia or Walla Walla onions, if available)
1 tablespoon sugar
2 tablespoons flour
1 cup dry or semi-dry white wine (chenin blanc, chablis, dry
   vermouth, or white table wine)
½ teaspoon freshly ground black pepper
1½ teaspoons salt
1 loaf French bread, sliced into ¾-inch-thick rounds
Enough slices of Swiss or Gruyère cheese to cover each bowl of
   soup

In a roasting pan, roast the soup bones in a preheated 450 degree oven for about 35 minutes. While roasting the bones, bring the water to a boil and maintain the boil, covered, until the bones are ready. Add the roasted bones to the boiling water (discard the rendered fat that will have collected on the roasting pan). Simmer the bones, covered, for a minimum of 2 hours.

While the bones are simmering, melt the butter and both oils in a large frying pan or brazier. Brush the tops of the bread slices with the butter mixture, spread the slices on a baking sheet, and put them in a preheated 300 degree oven to toast, for about 20 minutes. Set aside to cool.

In a large frying pan or heavy-bottomed pot, sauté the onions in the remaining butter/oil mixture over medium-high heat until soft and translucent. Add the sugar, and continue to cook until the onions caramelize (they will turn golden brown). This should take about 30 minutes. Do not leave the onions during this stage, but stir steadily. When the onions turn deep golden brown, stir in the flour until it disappears. Remove the pan from heat and set it aside.

Remove the bones from the broth with a slotted spoon. Using a gravy separator or "souper skimmer" (page 111), strain out all fat from the broth. Transfer the onion mixture to the broth. Add the wine, pepper, and add salt. Adjust the seasonings to taste.

Place 1 crouton on the bottom of each soup bowl. (This soup should be served in individual crock-style bowls, with a narrower width, rather than in a large serving bowl or wide-mouthed soup bowls.) Ladle the soup over the crouton, filling the bowl to ½ inch from the top. Float another crouton on top. Cover the bowl with sliced cheese. Place the bowl under the broiler or in a hot oven long enough for the cheese to melt over the top of the soup. Serve immediately.

ஃ Potato Cheese Soup

SERVES 8

This is a rich, creamy, comfort-food kind of soup. With a loaf of fresh bread, this is a meal unto itself.

1 quart chicken stock (page 113) or canned broth
2½ pounds potatoes, unpeeled but coarsely chopped
2 bunches scallions, diced
1 quart half-and-half, milk, or low-fat milk
4 tablespoons tamari (soy sauce)
1 teaspoon freshly ground black pepper
¾ pound Swiss or Cheddar cheese (or a combination), grated
1 cup dry white wine or beer (optional)
Paprika and fresh parsley sprigs for garnish

In a heavy-bottomed soup pot bring the chicken stock to a boil. Add the potatoes and simmer for 30 minutes. Add the scallions and remove the pot from the heat. Add the half-and-half or milk to the pot.

Purée the potato-broth mixture in a blender (when blending hot mixtures, fill blender only half full and cover the blender lid with a dish towel to protect against steam burns). Return the purée to the pot. Add the tamari and pepper and slowly bring the soup back to a simmer.

When the soup begins to simmer, stir in the grated cheese. It will melt very quickly. The addition of wine or beer, at this point, is a flavoring option. As soon as the cheese has melted, remove the soup from the heat and serve.

To serve, ladle the soup into large soup bowls. Sprinkle each serving with a little paprika and garnish with a sprig of parsley on top.

૨⚫ Susan's Vegetable Soup

SERVES 8

True vegetable penicillin, this soup is used by Susan as a viable alternative to chicken soup—to heal just about anything.

¼ pound butter or ½ cup vegetable oil (optional)
3 carrots, sliced and quartered
3 onions, coarsely chopped
3 potatoes, sliced and chopped into bite-size pieces
2 cups coarsely chopped cabbage
3 stalks celery, sliced
¼ pound mushrooms, halved or quartered
4 tomatoes, diced, or 1 can (28 ounces) crushed tomatoes with juice
15 cloves fresh garlic, minced
2 tablespoons dried basil
4 whole bay leaves
10 cups water
½ cup vegetarian chicken-flavored soup base (page 110)
¼ cup tamari (soy sauce)
½ teaspoon freshly ground black pepper
½ cup minced fresh parsley, plus sprigs for garnish (optional)
1 tablespoon grated fresh ginger

If using butter or oil, melt it in a heavy-bottomed soup pot. Add all the vegetables, except parsley, and the garlic, and sauté for 3 minutes. Add the basil, bay leaves, and water and bring it to a boil. (If omitting butter and oil, just bring all the ingredients above to a boil.)

When the water comes to a boil, stir in the soup base, tamari, black pepper, and ginger. Simmer for 30 minutes, or until the potatoes are soft. Taste and adjust the seasonings, using either more soup base, tamari, or salt.

Just before serving, mix in the parsley. You may also garnish the bowl with sprigs of parsley.

ও Spanish Lentil and Sausage Soup

SERVES 8

A wonderfully hearty winter soup. I originally wanted to call it "Esau Sells His Birthright Soup" because I could imagine Jacob making something like this centuries ago, but the name was too radical. This was one of many dishes we made with Bruce Aidells's fabulous chaurice Creole sausage, but if you cannot find it you may substitute chorizo or linguica. As with many of the "meated" soups, you can make a vegetarian version by simply substituting vegetarian soup base and adding some spices— paprika, cayenne, a touch of vinegar, and black pepper.

8 cups water
2 cups (1 pound) uncooked green lentils, washed and picked
   through for stones
1 teaspoon vegetable oil
2 pounds Creole sausage, linguica, or chorizo, chopped into
   small pieces
2 onions, diced
8 cloves garlic, minced
20 ounces frozen chopped spinach (two 10-ounce packages) or
   8 cups tightly packed chopped fresh spinach

4 large tomatoes, diced, or 1 can (28 ounces) diced or crushed
  tomatoes with juice
Chopped fresh parsley or cilantro for garnish

In a soup pot, bring the water to a boil, add the lentils, cover, and simmer for about 1 hour, or until the lentils are soft and splitting. Stir the pot periodically to prevent sticking and burning.

While the lentils are cooking, heat a frying pan, add the vegetable oil, and sauté the sausage until crisp and brown. Remove the sausage but leave the oil. In it sauté the onions and garlic for 3 minutes, or until the onions become translucent. Remove from the heat.

When the lentils are ready, add the sausage mixture with the oil. Then add the spinach and tomatoes. Bring the soup to a simmer and cook it for 10 minutes before serving. Garnish each serving with either chopped parsley or cilantro.

❧ Split Pea Soup with Ham Hocks

SERVES 8

Ham hocks are one of the true "secret ingredients" of cooking. They impart so much flavor and texture that I am surprised they are not more widely used. Great split pea soup can be made without them, but incredible split pea soup is made possible by their inclusion. If you leave out the ham hocks, there is a vegetarian smoked ham-flavored soup base available in some markets, which can give you a hint of what the ham hocks add. You can also add a few drops of liquid smoke.

18 cups water

4 cups (2 pounds) uncooked split peas, washed and checked for stones

2 pounds smoked ham hocks

4 tablespoons vegetable oil

1 carrot, diced

2 onions, diced

10 cloves fresh garlic, minced

4 bay leaves

1 tablespoon dried basil

1 tablespoon dried marjoram

1 teaspoon freshly ground black pepper

2 teaspoons salt, or to taste (The ham hocks are salty, so salt judiciously.)

Parsley sprigs for garnish

In a heavy-bottomed soup pot, bring 10 cups of the water to a boil and add the split peas. Cover and simmer over low heat for 1½ to 2 hours, or until the peas break down and dissolve. Stir the pot periodically to prevent sticking and burning. If the water seems to disappear, add a little more, enough to cover the peas.

At the same time, in a separate pot, bring the remaining 8 cups water to a boil, add the ham hocks, cover, and simmer for 2 hours. Strain the water and add it to the split peas after they have dissolved. Pick the meat off the hocks and discard the bones. Chop the meat and add it to the split peas and water. Continue cooking over low heat.

While the peas and hocks are cooking, heat the oil in a frying pan and sauté the carrot, onion, and garlic until the onion is translucent, about 5 minutes. Add the bay leaves, basil, and marjoram, stir for 1 more minute, and remove the pot from the heat.

When the split peas have broken down, add the salt, pepper, and carrot/onion mixture. The soup should be thick and creamy. Taste, adjust the seasonings, and cook over low heat for 10 minutes before serving, stirring frequently to allow the flavors to blend. Garnish the soup with fresh parsley sprigs.

Soups on the Wall

We made a number of blender soups at Brother Juniper's. The most important thing I learned about blender soups is to either let the soup cool before blending or, if blending hot soup, drape a towel over the top of the blender and start on a slow speed, with an escape vent for the steam. Hold the lid down lightly, under the towel, but allow it to pop up a little when the pressure forces it. Another technique is to remove the plastic center of the blender lid. The towel absorbs the spray of steam and liquid, and your hands will be spared a vicious steam burn. Believe me, I learned this trick the hard way.

There were times when some of the kids who worked for us did not take this instruction seriously enough, which is why I think of these as soups on the wall. You should not have this problem if you follow the advice above.

The "cream of" soups following are variations on a theme— they are all called "cream of" something. The foundation and concept of each soup is similiar but the flavors are unique.

❧ Cream of Broccoli Soup

SERVES 8

4 cups water

2 pounds fresh or frozen broccoli florets (discard lower stems
at the point where they seem to become woody), washed and
chopped into 1-inch pieces
3 potatoes unpeeled but coarsely chopped
2 onions, coarsely chopped
½ bunch chopped parsley
6 cloves garlic, peeled
½ teaspoon freshly ground black pepper
1 cup vegetarian chicken-flavored soup base (page 110; you
may substitute 4 cups real chicken stock for the soup base. If
so, use the stock in place of the 4 cups water and adjust the
salt at the end)
4 cups half-and-half, milk, or low-fat milk
½ cup dry or semi-dry white wine
Salt or tamari (soy sauce), to taste
Parsley sprigs for garnish

Put the water, broccoli, potatoes, onions, parsley, and garlic
in a soup pot. Bring the water to a boil, cover, and simmer for 30
to 40 minutes, or until the potatoes are soft. Remove the pot
from the heat. Add the black pepper and soup base.

Purée the mixture in a blender until smooth, making sure
that there is enough liquid from the pot so as not to strain the
blender motor. (If you need more liquid, use some of the half-
and-half or milk.) Return the purée to the pot and bring it to a
simmer.

Stir in the half-and-half or milk. Add the wine. Bring the
soup back to a simmer, adjust the seasoning (salt or tamari, to
taste), and serve. Garnish with parsley sprigs.

ஐ Cream of Green Soup

SERVES 8

Follow the directions and ingredients for Cream of Broccoli Soup, substituting 20 ounces of fresh chard or spinach in place of the broccoli and adding 1 teaspoon dried marjoram, basil, or oregano.

ஐ Cream of Celery Soup

SERVES 8

Follow the directions for Cream of Broccoli Soup, substituting 2 pounds of celery, sliced, for the broccoli. Also add 1 teaspoon of dried basil, marjoram, or oregano.

Because celery has fibrous strings, it is advisable to strip them off before cooking. This is done by snapping the very bottom of each stalk, revealing the strings. Using the snapped piece, still attached by the strings, strip the celery by moving it up the stalk, pulling the strings out as it goes.

After puréeing the soup, it will still be somewhat fibrous. Run it through a strainer or food mill, which will eliminate the celery strings, leaving a smooth, green soup.

❧ Cream of Watercress Soup

SERVES 6

¼ pound butter
3 large onions, coarsely chopped
3 stalks celery, stripped (see Cream of Celery Soup), and
  coarsely chopped
1 teaspoon black peppercorns
5 potatoes, unpeeled but diced
6 cups chicken broth (or 1 cup vegetarian chicken-flavored
  soup base dissolved in 5 cups water)
2 cups washed fresh watercress leaves
5 large cloves garlic, chopped
Salt, to taste
Nasturtium flowers for garnish

Melt the butter in a soup pot. Add the onions, celery, and peppercorns. Sauté over medium heat until the vegetables soften, then add the potatoes and broth. Bring to a boil and simmer for about 20 minutes, or until the potatoes are soft.

Add the watercress and garlic and simmer for about 2 minutes, or until the watercress wilts. Remove the pot from the heat.

Purée the entire mixture in a blender. Strain out any remaining remaining fibers through a food mill or strainer to make a smooth cream. Add salt to taste.

Serve garnished with nasturtium flowers, which are an edible flower in the watercress family, and have a slight peppery taste.

Cold Soups

During the summer we made a number of cold soups. The most popular were gazpacho and creamy avocado.

Gazpacho means "salad soup." It is one of the most refreshing and nourishing of all soups, with a salsa-like flavor and satisfaction. There have been days when I consumed two quarts of it myself. It is best when made with garden fresh vegetables at the peak of their bright colors.

The avocado soup was one of Susan's most popular. It is rich and creamy, but cool and refreshing, like a smooth guacamole. It is best eaten within twenty-four hours, while the flavors are fresh.

❧ Gazpacho

SERVES 6

8 medium vine-ripened tomatoes or two 28-ounce cans peeled
 Italian tomatoes (Do not use store-ripened tomatoes—they
 do not have enough flavor.)
¼ red onion, chopped
1 fresh jalapeño or serrano pepper, chopped
2 sweet bell peppers (green or red), chopped
8 cloves garlic, peeled
1 teaspoon dried oregano
⅔ cup olive oil
1 tablespoon red wine vinegar
¼ cup balsamic vinegar
1 teaspoon salt
¼ teaspoon freshly ground black pepper
1 cucumber, peeled and diced
1 bunch scallions, sliced into ¼-inch pieces
Croutons for garnish (page 37)

If using fresh tomatoes, blanch them in boiling water for 1 minute, then transfer them to a tub of cold water. Remove and peel off the skins.

Set aside the croutons, cucumber pieces, and half of the scallions.

Purée all the remaining ingredients in a blender. Transfer to a bowl. Stir in the cucumber and scallion pieces and chill. To serve, ladle into individual bowls and sprinkle 6 or 7 croutons on top as a garnish.

❧ Creamy Avocado Soup

SERVES 6

1 quart half-and-half or low-fat milk
1 quart chicken broth, at room temperature (You may substitute 4 tablespoons vegetarian chicken-flavored soup base [page 110], dissolved in 2 cups water.)
5 large ripe avocados, pitted and peeled
¼ small onion
½ cup fresh lemon juice
½ cup fresh lime juice
1 teaspoon salt
¾ teaspoon freshly ground white or black pepper
4 tablespoons finely chopped chives for garnish
Lime slices cut into thin coin-shaped pieces for garnish

Purée all the ingredients except the chives and lime slices until smooth and creamy. If the soup is too thick, thin it down with milk or water. Chill for 1 hour, or until the soup is cold.

Ladle the soup into bowls and garnish with a sprinkle of chives and a thin slice of lime.

NOTE: If storing overnight, do not leave lime slices in the soup as the rind will impart a bitter flavor. You may, however, follow an old folk custom and leave a few avocado pits in the soup, which will help it keep its green color.

BARBECUE

Holy Smoke

I am a member of an unofficial fraternity consisting of the world's greatest barbecue sauce makers. Believing that I should be the only member fulfills one of the criteria of membership. That each of us stands convinced and unmoveable in our prideful fanaticism is another criterion. Finally, despite this unshakeable belief in the superiority of my own sauce, I endlessly search out other brands and homemade variations, another membership prerequisite. We are a small but predictable group; perhaps we are a cult, albeit a benevolent one, not unlike the cult of chili fanatics who have somehow managed to organize themselves into the International Chili Society.

At a tasting event last year a man approached our booth, where we were giving out tastes of barbecue sauce on slices of our bread. Before trying anything he bragged a little about how he made the greatest barbecue sauce from a secret family recipe. He then ate a little dab of our sauce on a piece of bread and his head shot up involuntarily. Inwardly I smiled, not wanting to reveal my lack of surprise. Holy Smoke had claimed another convert.

"Hey, that's pretty good," he said in classic understated tones. To a member of *the club* his words really meant, "Whoa! I've been put to shame. You have outperformed me. I concede!" He then committed the final act of submission—he bought a jar. His act of humility, in a way, shamed me because he demonstrated a deep truth: being a member of my exclusive clique lacks all virtue. It is the bittersweet paradox of the hollow victory. It is Holly Hunter, in *Broadcast News,* confronted by her boss who says, sarcastically, "It must be great always being the smartest one in the room, always being right," while Holly mournfully replies, "No, it's not. It's awful." I belong to a club in which, in a variation of Groucho's maxim, I should be ashamed to be a member. But I'm not.

The seeds of Holy Smoke were sown when I was a youth. At the age of ten I had already decided that my greatest joy in life came from eating barbecued chicken. My Uncle Sam, who summered every year in Atlantic City, offered to take me to any restaurant on the Boardwalk. I chose the all-you-can-eat barbecued chicken restaurant near the Steel Pier. I have since amended my values and priorities a bit but the damage was done, I fear, early and irrevocably. A passion for barbecue has trailed and haunted me ever since those formative years. Even during my staunchest counterculture period, my strictest vegetarian stage, and my firmest renunciation of the past I have loved barbecue in every way, shape, or form.

It was a visit to Flint's Barbecue in Oakland, California, that finally put me over the edge. I had recently finished reading Calvin Trillin's trilogy of food books in which he canonizes Arthur Bryant and his barbecue joint in Kansas City. Simultaneously, a local reviewer wrote about Flint's and said it was even better than Arthur Bryant's. The gauntlet having been thrown, I was drawn into the drama like a fly on, well, barbecue sauce. It took only five minutes to coax some fellow barbecue "cultists" to jump in a car with me and make the thirty-minute drive over the

Bay Bridge to the Fruitvale section of Oakland, a place I would not ordinarily go unless under the spell of some powerful force or aroma.

Being first-timers we thought we would eat there but, as Gertrude Stein has been oft quoted about Oakland, "There is no there there." There, in this case, was an upstairs room that few had the courage, or ignorance, to use. Trusting in God and the security guard, we stumbled upstairs, hugging our precious cargo of hot links, brisket, chicken, and ribs, trying not to spill our drinks or otherwise embarrass ourselves.

Our dinner conversation revolved around the wood-fired "pit," which, when briefly opened to extract the meat, revealed gorgeous racks of ribs, strings of links, spits of chickens, and hunks of hanging beef brisket, blackened to tear-inducing beauty, teasing us into premature salivation. When the counter person *whacked* out our various portions with his giant cleaver, then poured the precious "secret" barbecue sauce over the whole thing, we felt like dervish sufis after a six-hour whirl of chanting and spinning. We opened our butcher-paper bundles in the "dining room," ignoring the stains and sticky spots on the table as the trance held. Each package was like a treasure, a pearl of great price, and we buzzed like drones pointing out little discoveries to each other. "Oh look, here's a whole pile of burnt edges!" or, "These links, these links . . . oh my God, I've never tasted anything like this in my life!"

It was, in retrospect, quite embarrassing. It was also one of the best meals I ever had, the manifestation of the vision I had had at ten years of age in Atlantic City, in which the streets of heaven had a barbecue joint on every corner. You may laugh at me, and you should, but for a few fleeting minutes the Fruitvale section of Oakland was about as close to paradise as I had ever been. The implications of this statement I intend to develop at another time, in another book.

It was during this meal that I saw what I had to do. At the risk of becoming like Richard Dreyfuss in *Close Encounters of the Third Kind* building a Devil's Mountain out of mashed potatoes, topsoil, and garden shrubs, I became obsessed with the mission of creating a barbecue sauce that was even better than Flint's. It took me five years but, by God, I did it. I cannot claim that it has brought me inner peace or contentment, but it has brought me many fine meals.

The challenge to accomplishing this goal was made quite clear a few months after my first visit when I returned to Flint's. I was met by a large black woman, wearing a platinum wig and acting for all the world as if she must be Mrs. Flint herself. Rarely have I seen such authority and certainty displayed, and I can never think of her without calling her Mama Flint, even if that is not who she was. She took my order while three youngsters served it up. I was alone and wanted to take some brisket and ribs back for my friends in San Francisco. I made the almost fatal mistake of asking for extra sauce on the beef.

"There's enough sauce on there," Mama Flint said.

"I'll pay extra for some more sauce or even a cup of sauce on the side," I bravely said back.

"You don't understand," said Mama Flint, her awesome size and authority rising up in front of me. "That's all the sauce you get. There's enough sauce on there for you and anybody else."

I took the big risk: "Are you afraid someone's going to try to duplicate it?"

"Honey," she said, as she turned to the three youngsters, two girls and a boy, "there's all manner of people out there trying to duplicate this here sauce."

The three kids suddenly became like a gospel chorus, responding to her as if she were Mahalia Jackson. "Oh yeah!" they said in unison.

"They try!" said Mama Flint.

"Oh yeah, they try!" came the chorus.

"Oh honey, they try, yeah they try!"

"Tell him, Mama, they try!" came the litany.

Her more than ample bosom was shaking like Jell-O as she bounced up and down before me and in front of her praise the Lord chorus. "They try and they try and they try. But you know what, honey?"

Silence.

Then the chorus said, in a whisper, "Tell him, Mama."

Another long pause, as I looked at Mama Flint, then back to the three who were all smiling, and sweating, and filled with a rapture that I've seen only a few times in a few churches. "Tell him, Mama."

"THEY FAIL!" came the climactic words. "OH, THEY FAIL!"

"Yeah, they try but they fail, they try but they fail! And that's the truth, Mama."

And then she put my package of barbecue in front of me and said, "That'll be $8.75. You want anything else?"

"That oughta do it," I whispered, as I backed out, intimidated and exhilarated. But I knew, Mama Flint notwithstanding, I was not going to fail.

The first batch was ready just in time for Christmas, so we bottled some up and sent it to friends and family for the holidays. The response was terrific. My mother called from Philadelphia to tell me she had come up with the perfect name: Holy Smoke. At first I was put off, thinking it somewhat irreverent, but then I started to chuckle. Here I was, living in a semimonastic religious community, making barbecue sauce as a hobby. There was not much room for self-righteousness in such a context. *Holy Smoke* captured the irony of the situation perfectly and Holy Smoke it became. Thanks, Mom.

Flint's in Fruitvale is only a few blocks from the Oakland Coliseum, where the Golden State Warriors play their home games. Once a year a group of us bought tickets to a game and made the ninety-minute drive from Forestville. (I had moved to our retreat center in Forestville shortly after the "They try but they fail" episode.) We always arrived early enough to stop at Flint's and pick up some barbecue for a tailgate dinner at the arena. I made it a habit to bring with me a cup of the most recent incarnation of Holy Smoke for comparison purposes. We first took a bite of Flint's, then dipped into my sauce. Then we critiqued. For four years the comments boiled down to, "You're getting close." On the fifth year, just months before the opening of Brother Juniper's Café, we went through the ritual again. After the initial comparison there was quiet in the car. Finally someone said, "I need to try that again." I knew what that meant for even I noticed it. Something was different.

"Do you think they changed their sauce?" I asked.

"No, it's just as good as always," came the hoped-for reply. This could mean only one thing.

We consumed the meal in silence, broken only by the customary and involuntary sighs of pleasure that are always induced by Flint's barbecue. Then we packed up, wiping our faces with the wet napkins we learned to bring with us. After locking the car and heading into the Coliseum, somebody said quietly, respectfully, "I think you've done it."

There was, again, a quiet chorus of assent from the others. My ego was not stroked, as I expected, but an almost reverential quality of awe enveloped us as we experienced the passing of the torch. They try, Mama Flint, but they don't always fail.

Since we are beginning to sell Holy Smoke all over the country, I cannot reveal the exact, still-secret formula (oh the irony!). But here are some variations of Holy Smoke Barbecue Sauce, and how to best use them:

‏‏‎ Red Barbecue Sauce

MAKES 10 CUPS

2 cans (28 ounces each) tomato purée
8 cloves fresh garlic, pressed
1 medium onion, diced
4½ cups white sugar
2 cups red wine vinegar
5 tablespoons Worcestershire sauce
5 tablespoons liquid smoke (available at most supermarkets)
¾ cup light molasses
½ cup Brother Juniper's Chile Peppermash (page 6) or 4
   tablespoons Tabasco
½ teaspoon freshly ground black pepper
1 tablespoon salt
½ cup fresh lemon juice

Combine all ingredients, except the lemon juice, in a large pot and bring to a boil. Simmer for 10 minutes, turn off the heat, then add the lemon juice. Use more peppermash or hot sauce to increase the heat, if desired. Store in the refrigerator; it will keep indefinitely.

❧ Honey Sweetened Barbecue Sauce

Make as above, substituting 5 cups honey for the white sugar.

❧ Blond Barbecue Sauce
Mustard-based South Carolina–Style

Substitute 5 cups prepared mustard (regular ballpark style) for the tomato purée, and cut the vinegar to 1 cup. Prepare as above. Sweeten with either sugar or honey.

Specific Types of Barbecue

꿈 When Brother Juniper's Café opened we served five types of barbecue: brisket, spareribs, hot links, chicken, and marinated tofu. A year later, when it became clear that the most ardent barbecue fans were the vegetarians, we added tempeh. We then added roast pork following the suggestion of our friend and quality meat supplier Nate DelQuerro, who pointed out that tender pork slices perfectly complemented Holy Smoke because they would soak up lots of sauce. The barbecued pork became a big hit.

We were not able to smoke foods in our café because of fire code regulations. This may have been a healthy benefit, now that so much about smoking meats has come under question, but it was the one drawback to the creating of perfect barbecue. To compensate, we used liquid smoke in the sauce, which has one thing strongly in its favor: the carcinogenic elements of smoke are filtered out during the distillation process. It must be used in moderation, though, or it imparts a bitter, acrid flavor into the sauce.

Rather than slow smoking the meats over wood or coals, we devised our own methods of cooking, which are easy to replicate at home. The goal was to serve moist and juicy meat that would act like a sponge for the sauce. With tofu and tempeh, two rather bland soybean-based foods, the challenge was to build into the product some complementary flavors. This is accomplished through marinades, which are given in another chapter (page 5). It is important to remember that all of these foods can be prepared on a grill, over coals or lava rocks, to great advantage. But the following is for indoor cooking with the emphasis on juiciness. If you want to grill whole roasts over coals, please refer to any number of excellent grilling books (most high-quality grills such as Ducane and Weber provide very good grilling instructions in the grill manuals). The key is very slow, even cooking, which gives the deepest, smokiest flavor.

Beef Brisket

Preheat your oven to 325 degrees. Place a whole brisket (4 or more pounds) in a roasting pan. Cover the top with any commercial dry onion soup mix (the kind that makes great onion dip works well; it will take 2 packets). Put 1 cup of water in the bottom of the pan. Cover the top of the pan with aluminum foil, making sure it is sealed all around the edges to keep the steam in. Roast for approximately 2½ hours, or 35 minutes for each pound of beef. When finished cooking, allow it to sit in the covered pan for an additional 20 minutes before removing the foil.

Slice the brisket thinly, saving all the juice, occasionally basting the brisket slices with the juice. If serving immediately, place a few slices of beef on a slice of fresh French bread, ladle a little of the juice over it, then ladle warm barbecue sauce over all.

If grilling, put the slices of precooked brisket on the grill, brush with the barbecue sauce, and grill for 1 minute on each side. Ladle more sauce on the beef after it is transferred to the plates, as above.

N O T E : To tenderize the beef further, simmer slices in the pan juices for 30 minutes. The beef should begin to fall apart, soaking up the juices. This is the most flavorful of all, and it will absorb the barbecue sauce like a sponge.

〰 Pork Roast

Prepare exactly as brisket, substituting any cut of pork roast. (We used pork butt.)

〰 Spareribs

Pork ribs can be prepared a number of ways. Some people like to boil or steam them first (to tenderize), then roast or grill them to finish. Susan met people in St. Louis who marinated their ribs overnight in beer, after first poking them with a fork. We dry-roasted our ribs and then steamed them in a Dutch oven to heat and tenderize. Remember to remove the inedible membrane that wraps itself around the rack (or have your butcher do it). If you have your own smoker, by all means use it. Otherwise, here are two methods of cooking:

Method 1

Submerge one or more racks of spareribs in boiling water for 45 minutes (or "steam-roast" for 1 hour, in a covered baking dish with 3 cups water at 400 degrees). Remove and drain.

Place the ribs in a hot oven (400 degrees), or under a broiler on a roasting pan, or directly on the barbecue grill. Brush on the barbecue sauce and turn the ribs over as soon as they begin to caramelize, grilling for about 3 to 5 minutes per side, charring equally on both sides.

Method 2

Preheat the oven to 350 degrees (300 if using a convection oven).

Rub a mixture of equal parts granulated garlic and coarse ground black pepper into the meaty side of uncooked ribs. Place in a baking pan and roast, uncovered, for 90 minutes, or until the ribs are golden brown and the fat is crisp and dark. Cut and separate the cooked ribs.

Then place the ribs in a deep pan or Dutch oven (a deep frying pan with a heavy, removeable lid) with 1 cup water. Cover and cook over high heat, steaming the ribs for 5 minutes. The meat should be ready to fall off the bone.

To serve, place the ribs on a plate and ladle warm barbecue sauce over the top. Remember to serve with fresh bread, coleslaw, and pickle. A sprig of parsley adds a nice touch.

≥ Hot Links

Our favorite link is Aidells chaurice Creole, the same smoked, spicy sausage that we used in our Spanish Lentil and Sausage Soup (page 118). Almost any good, spicy sausage will work—use your favorite. The cooking technique is simple:

Slice sausage(s) lengthwise, leaving hinged, so they form a long butterfly. Heat a skillet, add 1 teaspoon vegetable oil, and fry the sausages, cut side down, for about 3 minutes, over medium heat. Turn over and continue frying for another 2 minutes. The sausages should be charred on both sides. Remove from the pan onto thick paper towels to drain. Slice into thirds and place a few pieces on a slice of fresh French bread. Ladle warm barbecue sauce over the top, garnish with parsley, and serve with coleslaw and pickles.

≥ Chicken

Oven-baked chicken is delicious. Though it lacks the smokiness of barbecuing, it stays succulent and the smoky flavor is restored through the barbecue sauce. Here is how we made ours:

Preheat the oven to 350 degrees. Rub chicken pieces with a mixture of equal parts granulated garlic and coarse ground black pepper. Arrange the chicken on a roasting pan. Bake for 90 minutes, or until the pieces turn golden brown and the skin is crispy. The wings should be especially crisp and easy to pull apart; if they are not, the thicker pieces will be underdone. When done, remove the chicken from the oven and place on a platter. Ladle barbecue sauce over the top and garnish with parsley sprigs. Serve with fresh bread, coleslaw, and a good quality dill pickle.

≥ Tofu and Tempeh

These were very popular, and not only with vegetarians. Tempeh is a fermented soybean patty and is a good protein substitute for meat. It is pretty bland, but a few creative companies have learned how to marinate flavor into it. Our favorite, and the one we used at Brother Juniper's, is called "lemon broil." It is available at most natural food markets.

Tofu is a cheese-curd made from soy milk. It can be bought as regular, firm, or extra-firm. Use the firmest you can get; otherwise it falls apart in the marinade.

See page 5 for the marinade recipe. Cut the tofu into 1-inch squares and submerge them in the marinade for at least 24 hours. Keep the marinating tofu in the refrigerator until you are ready to use it.

Whether making barbecued tofu or tempeh, here is how to do it:

In a skillet or frying pan, heat 2 tablespoons vegetable oil until it sizzles when a drop of water is splashed in it. Add the tofu or tempeh pieces a few at a time and fry for about 3 minutes on each side, or until the pieces are crisp and golden brown. Remove to a thick paper towel to drain.

Arrange the tofu or tempeh on a slice of bread or directly on the plate. Ladle barbecue sauce over the top. Garnish with a sprig of parsley and serve with coleslaw and a pickle.

PASTA

&

MORE

Beyond Pasta

૨૭ Pasta is what I call the Saint Paul of foods: It is all things to all men. I realized we were in the midst of a pasta renaissance when I began to see squid ink pasta on the menus of every neo-Italian restaurant and in most of the fresh pasta shops that are becoming so popular. Since then I've seen all kinds of pasta on seemingly every menu in every restaurant. It has been touted as a great health food, gourmet food, diet food, peasant food, patrician food—let's face it, pasta is, without doubt, all things to all people. Is there a more perfect, versatile, flexible foundation for a meal? Probably not.

I love noodles, though I am not a true pasta fanatic (but Susan is). I have, however, made my share of fresh pasta over the years, which is almost as much fun as making bread. I am usually more interested, though, in the sauces that go over the noodles.

To my own amazement I have also discovered that when all the hubbub about the fresh pasta boom finally leveled out, my tastes had swung back toward dried pasta. There are times when the soft, fresh noodles are called for in a recipe, but for plain old spaghetti and its relatives I find the toothsome qualities of the dry pasta to be more enjoyable. Fresh pasta seems to work better, to my taste, in Oriental foods, or in the flat noodle dishes that

feature some other prominent item such as large pieces of seafood or unusual vegetables.

Susan and I collaborated on one pasta dish during the early
stages of what I call the "nuevo pasta era" and it became quite
popular. It combined our love of Cajun food, sauces, and noodles. It also featured a wonderful three-pepper pasta made by our
friends Bernard and Maria, who have a shop nearby called Pasta
Etc. The two key ingredients, besides the pasta, are good-quality
dried cheese (Parmesan, Romano, or even aged jack, which is a
fine domestic substitute) and tasso—a smokey spicy ham. The
preparation is somewhat complex because it has to be assembled
just before serving. It makes a wonderful entrée for company and
goes well with either light fruity wines (Gewürztraminer is my
choice) or beer. This dish is pretty to look at, exciting to the
palate, and makes a wonderful centerpiece for an intimate dinner. We used to call it Cajun Pasta but lately, when we make it at
home for ourselves or guests, I call it Beyond Pasta.

ɤ Beyond Pasta

SERVES FOUR

1 pound fresh or dried pasta (linguine, spaghetti, or fettuccine)
1 tablespoon cornstarch
2 cups chicken broth, at room temperature
½ cup extra-virgin olive oil
3 tablespoons butter
½ pound tasso (see Note below), julienned (sliced into small
  matchstick pieces)
 1 cup finely chopped fresh parsley

8 large cloves fresh garlic, finely minced
2 medium sweet red bell peppers, seeded and sliced into thin
    strips
¼ teaspoon coarsely ground black pepper
2 medium onions, sliced into half-moon strips
½ cup cream sherry
½ cup fresh lemon juice
½ pound freshly grated Parmesan, Romano, or aged jack cheese

NOTE: Tasso is hard to find. Ask your meat merchant to order some for you. The best brand is Aidells, which is made in San Francisco. Bruce Aidells suggests, if you cannot get tasso, to substitute smokey Westphalian ham (high in quality, but expensive) or directly contact Aidells Sausage Co., 1575 Minnesota Street, San Francisco, CA 94107 (415-285-6660). A less-expensive ham or Canadian bacon would also work. Here is a spice blend I make if I am out of tasso: 1½ tablespoons paprika, 1 tablespoon coarse garlic powder, 1 teaspoon cayenne, ½ teaspoon freshly ground black pepper. Toss the julienned ham in this mixture until coated. Use the spiced ham as you would tasso. (The spice blend will coat ½ pound of ham strips.)

Cook the pasta so that it will be ready at the same time as the sauce.

Dissolve the cornstarch in ¼ cup cold chicken broth and set aside.

In a frying pan, heat the olive oil and butter. Add the tasso or ham and sauté over medium-high heat till crisp, about 3 or 4 minutes. With a slotted spoon, remove the meat from the pan and set aside. Leave the oil in the pan.

Add the parsley, garlic, sweet peppers, black pepper, and onions to the pan and sauté till the onions are translucent and the peppers are bright red, about 5 minutes. Return the tasso to the pan and toss for 1 more minute. With a slotted spoon, re-move the onion/pepper/tasso mixture and set it aside, leaving all juices in the pan.

Add the remaining chicken broth (1¾ cups) and cream sherry to the pan. Bring to a boil and simmer the sauce for 2 minutes to reduce the liquid.

Whisk in the cornstarch mixture, bring the sauce back to a boil, add the lemon juice, and remove the pan from the heat.

Place the cooked hot pasta in a serving dish or pasta platter. Sprinkle half of the cheese over the pasta. Spread the onion/pepper/tasso mixture over the cheese. Pour the sauce over the entire dish. Finally, sprinkle the remaining cheese over the top and serve.

Some Other Pasta Options

Susan, pasta fanatic that she is, has been experimenting at home with some new pasta ideas. She inspired me to develop a few as well. The following are recipes that taste great and can be assembled quickly (to which I add one reminder: the fruit mari-nade/sauces on page 10 also make excellent pasta sauces when you are in the mood for something different and zippy!).

ᘔ Pasta Puttanesca

SERVES 4

I have been told by an Italian friend that puttanesca *refers to food of the red-light district. This is, without doubt, a lively, robust sauce, evoking the sights, sounds, and images of Fellini's* Nights of Cabiria. *Unlike most puttanesca sauces, this recipe is*

made without anchovies. I can also testify that it tastes good in
any light.

¼ cup extra-virgin olive oil
1 medium onion, finely diced
6 large cloves garlic, minced, plus 6 large cloves garlic, slivered
1 carrot, grated
½ cup chopped flat-leaf parsley
2 tablespoons dried oregano
Two 28-ounce cans good-quality whole peeled plum tomatoes
    with basil or an equal amount tomato purée (for a smoother
    sauce)
20 Greek Calamata olives
4 tablespoons olive juice
3 tablespoons capers
1 teaspoon salt
½ cup dry red table wine
Freshly grated Romano or Parmesan cheese, to taste
1 pound dried or fresh linguine or your favorite pasta, cooked
    according to the directions on the package

In a heavy-bottomed saucepan, heat the olive oil to medium
hot. When the oil begins to ripple, add the onion and stir until it
becomes translucent. Add the minced garlic and stir for 1 minute.
Add the grated carrot, parsley, and oregano and stir for 1 additional minute (you want the ingredients to burst their flavor in
the oil, but not to brown). Add the undrained tomatoes and
bring to a boil, stirring constantly.

Boil for 3 minutes, breaking up the tomatoes with a spoon
or a potato masher. Reduce the heat to medium, cover, and simmer for 1 hour, stirring occasionally.

Remove the lid, add the olives, olive juice, capers, slivered garlic, salt, and red wine. Simmer, uncovered, for ½ hour to reduce.

Prepare the pasta and serve topped with the sauce and a sprinkling of grated cheese.

🐚 Pasta Susan
"Wild" Mushrooms, Pan-Fried Garlic, and Wine Sauce

SERVES 4

We live at the southern tip of the northwestern wild mushroom zone, which extends from Sonoma County northward into Oregon and Washington. This is serendipitous since Susan and I, like so many others, simply love wild mushrooms. We have done a little mushroom foraging in the woods of Forestville, where boletus edulus *(porcini) mushrooms reign supreme. But heeding the ancient axiom, "There are old mushroom hunters and there are bold mushroom hunters, but there are no old bold mushroom hunters," we usually buy ours at the farmer's market. There, they have been picked within twenty-four hours, usually in the Mendocino Forest, by professional foragers who may cover up to fifteen miles a night looking for the rarest, most valuable fungi.*

There are also cultivated "wild" mushrooms available in many markets. The shiitake *mushroom, which is usually associated with Oriental cuisine, has now become somewhat commonplace, but also more affordable. Oyster mushrooms are fairly tame in flavor, but they soak up the flavors of the sauces in which they are served. Occasionally you may discover* portobello *mushrooms in the market. These are large brown and black over-*

grown cremini mushrooms and may cost up to $6.00 a pound. At that price they better be as good as filet mignon, and they are when marinated, grilled, and served by themselves.

There are now even frozen wild mushrooms, as well as the more well-known dried mushrooms found in Oriental sections of the market. However you get them, once you begin to cook with wild mushrooms they can become an expensive habit.

This recipe is a good showcase for the easily obtained culti-vated wild mushrooms such as shiitake *and* oyster. *The flavors are nicely counterpointed by the crisp garlic slices and the tangy wine and lemon–reduction sauce. The sauce has a beautiful burgundy-rose color from the wine. We have learned to keep the mushrooms separate from the other ingredients lest their unique, delicate flavor disappear in the sauce.*

1 pound angel hair pasta or linguine (You can use lemon-pepper pasta for an extra flavor boost.)
¼ cup extra-virgin olive oil
1 head garlic (approximately 15 cloves), peeled and cut into thin slices (cut lengthwise, not across, to get long slices)
¾ teaspoon salt
½ pound fresh wild or "cultivated" wild mushrooms, cut into thick slices (use *shiitake,* oyster, or cremini—but not *chanterelles,* which are too expensive and delicate for this dish; nor portobellos, which give off a dark juice that will discolor the sauce)
2½ cups red Burgundy or a good table wine
1 cup fresh lemon juice
4 dried hot chile peppers, coarsely chopped
¼ teaspoon coarsely ground black pepper
6 tablespoons butter
½ cup freshly grated Parmesan or Romano cheese
¼ cup minced fresh parsley

Cook the pasta according to the instructions on the package. Time it to be finished just after the reduction of the sauce (see below).

Set up a small strainer over a bowl. Heat a frying pan to medium-hot. When hot, add the olive oil. When the oil is hot, add the sliced garlic. Stir constantly to prevent burning, and sauté for 3 to 4 minutes, or until the garlic turns golden and crisp. Stir in ¼ teaspoon of salt. Pour the garlic, salt, and oil through the strainer, making sure to get all the garlic out of the pan (if the garlic burns it will make the sauce bitter). Return the oil to the pan and set the garlic aside. Turn the heat to high.

Stir-fry the mushrooms in the oil. They will absorb most of the oil and cook quickly (slow cooking causes the mushrooms to release their juices, which you do not want to happen). After about 3 minutes, the mushrooms should begin to brown. Remove them from the pan to a bowl.

Return the pan to high heat and add the wine. When the wine bubbles and foams it will begin to reduce. When about half has evaporated (after about 4 minutes), add the lemon juice, chopped chile peppers, black pepper, and the remaining ½ teaspoon salt. Continue to reduce the sauce for about 3 minutes, or until it begins to thicken. Reduce the heat to medium and add the butter. Cook until the butter melts, then remove the sauce from the heat. This will make about 1½ cups of a smooth, creamy, burgundy-colored sauce. (This step takes approximately 7 to 8 minutes; see Note below.)

Drain the pasta and transfer to a bowl or pasta plate. Pour the sauce over the pasta and toss to coat thoroughly. Add the mushrooms and toss again. Spread the grated cheese over the pasta, sprinkle on the sliced garlic, and then finish the presentation with the minced parsley. Serve immediately.

NOTE: Do not take your attention from this sauce to attend to the pasta or anything else, as it can quickly reduce too much and burn. When the sauce is finished, remove it from the heat and then deal with the pasta, which should be timed to be almost ready.

✑ Pasta with *Chèvre* and Sun-Dried Tomatoes

SERVES 4

Goat cheese is gaining in popularity due to the efforts of people like Steven Schack, Jennifer Bice, and Laura Chenel. They are among the dozens of cheese makers who helped educate the American palate during the past ten years with world-class chèvres *and other goat milk cheeses.*

It is interesting that the growth of the goat cheese industry has paralleled the discovery of marinated sun-dried tomatoes. A few years ago we used to make a few gallons to give, in small jars, as holiday gifts. Since then sun-dried tomatoes have become so common and easily available that we have had to come up with new gift ideas.

This recipe combines the best of both ingredients. It is a tangy and visually beautiful dish, taking full advantage of the concentrated flavor qualities of the marinated tomatoes.

Sauce
½ cup extra-virgin olive oil
6 large cloves fresh garlic, peeled
½ cup fresh lemon juice
4 ounces *chèvre* (goat cheese, available in gourmet or specialty food markets, or in many supermarkets)
6 marinated sun-dried tomatoes, drained of excess marinade
2 large fresh basil leaves

1 teaspoon mixed peppercorns (available in gourmet or
specialty food markets, or in many supermarkets)
1 teaspoon salt or kosher salt
> *Topping*
6 marinated sun-dried tomatoes, drained and cut into thin
strips
½ cup freshly grated Parmesan or Romano cheese
6 or 7 fresh basil leaves

1 pound lemon-pepper fettuccine or your favorite pasta

Make the sauce: Put all of the sauce ingredients in a blender or food processor and blend until smooth and creamy.

Prepare the topping ingredients: Do not cut the basil into chiffonade until just prior to serving. To cut the basil into chiffonade, stack the leaves 6 or 7 high and roll up like a cigar, across (not down) the center vein. Starting at one end, slice the rolled leaves into thin strips; unfurl. Cut basil browns (oxidizes) quickly, so this step should be performed just before serving.

Cook and drain the pasta, transfer to a serving bowl or pasta plate, and pour on all the sauce. Toss well to coat thoroughly.

Sprinkle on the cheese, then the tomato and basil strips. Serve immediately.

NOTE: Make sure all ingredients are at room temperature. If chilled, the sauce will cool down the dish too quickly.

Ratatouille, or Cleaning Up

at Fetzer

❧ I had a great learning experience during "The American Regional Food Festival" held at Fetzer Winery in Hopland, California, in the fall of 1990. It brought together many well-known chefs from all over the country, each demonstrating distinctive and original cuisines inspired by products of their region. The guest of honor was Julia Child.

All of the guest chefs presented classes, teaching the lucky audience of about two hundred not only techniques of cooking but also the thinking behind their styles. It was a wonderful opportunity to get a sense of why foods from various regions are different, how styles evolve, and the forces that shape a cuisine. It was also a glimpse into how chefs connect to the meaning of their work and the sense of mission that drives them. The high point of the day was a feast of all the dishes demonstrated by each of the guest chefs.

I volunteered to help, thinking I would shuck oysters or clean greens. But John Ash, the culinary director at Fetzer and one of Brother Juniper's good friends and supporters, arranged for me to have what turned out to be the best job imaginable for a budding chef: I got to clean up after each of the cooking demonstrations. This meant I was able to taste everything right after it was made and talk with the chefs who had prepared it. This made me, for months afterward, the envy of all my foodie friends. It also introduced me to Julia Child, who taught a class on ratatouille, a casserole of eggplant, zucchini, tomatoes, and other vegetables and herbs. While all the other chefs presented "original" regional recipes, Julia prepared a "classic" dish, one that could be found in practically any cookbook. She said, and Susan and I repeat this whenever we get into culinary discussions, that it is more important to make classic dishes properly (which means deliciously, with the best available ingredients, following fundamental principles), than to keep trying to come up with new concoctions just for the sake of originality. Ratatouille, she pointed out, should be in every cook's repertoire because it challenges us to bring out the best flavors of the fresh ingredients, building a foundation in basic culinary skills.

I refer to this experience at Fetzer as "my cleaning up after Julia day." It confirmed my feeling that there are depths to plumb in many ordinary dishes that we take for granted, and that it is not simply the creativity of the cook that contributes to the possibility of magic. Quality, not originality, is the trigger. It unlocks the door of all possibilities. Thank you, Julia.

Ratatouille

SERVES 4 TO 8

Julia Child has her own recipe for this dish but there are, legitimately, many ways to prepare and serve ratatouille. It is often presented as a side dish to accompany barbecued meats, sausages, or fowl. I have also served it as a main course, the casserole entrée of a vegetarian meal. Some recipes, such as Joël

*Robuchon's, suggest cutting the eggplant and zucchini into juli-
enne strips, giving the dish a relish or caponata look. Others call
for long, thin slices artfully layered in geometric designs. Classic
does not always mean conformity.*

*The fundamental principle is to treat each of the vegetables
separately, rather than combining and cooking them into a stew
or ragout. Most recipes call for sautéing and then layering each
of the vegetables. It is possible, however, to stay true to the spirit
of this dish while adding yet another flavor dimension by grilling
the vegetables, rather than sautéing. This, I believe, turns what is
normally an underappreciated, utilitarian dish into a showstop-
per, both to the palate and to the eye. The preparation is more
time-consuming than many other versions, but the complex fire-
roasted flavors of the vegetables make it well worth the effort.*

1 cup olive oil
¼ cup balsamic vinegar
¼ cup fresh lemon juice
6 large cloves garlic, minced or pressed
1½ teaspoons salt
½ teaspoon freshly ground black pepper
1 medium-large eggplant (about 1 pound), unpeeled and sliced
   into rectangular strips ½ inch thick, 2 inches wide, and 3
   inches long
6 small zucchini or summer squash (about 1 pound), sliced
   lengthwise into slices ½ inch thick and 3 inches long
3 large green or red bell peppers, seeded and sliced into strips 1
   inch wide and 3 inches long
¼ pound large mushrooms, stemmed, saving the stems
 2 medium onions, unpeeled and halved lengthwise
1 bunch fresh basil leaves, coarsely chopped
3 tablespoons minced fresh thyme, marjoram, or oregano (or a
   combination of all three)

2 pounds vine-ripened tomatoes, sliced into ½-inch-thick
  rounds

While preparing the vegetables, fire-up a gas or charcoal
grill to high, or preheat the oven broiler.

Combine the olive oil, vinegar, lemon juice, garlic, salt, and
pepper in a large mixing bowl. Add the sliced eggplant, zucchini,
and the bell pepper strips and toss so that everything is coated.
Marinate for 5 minutes, then transfer the marinated vegetables to
a sieve or colander positioned over a large bowl. Allow them to
drain for 5 minutes, collecting the excess marinade and returning
it to the original bowl.

Grill or broil the vegetables for about 5 minutes on each
side, or until they are fully soft and slightly charred (it is helpful
to work with just one vegetable at a time, such as the eggplant, in
order to keep track). As the vegetables finish cooking, remove
them from the heat and set them on a large platter.

Toss the mushroom caps and stems, as well as the onion
halves, in the remaining marinade, just to coat them. Transfer
these to the grill or broiler and cook until tender. The mushrooms will take about 3 minutes on each side to brown and
soften. When they do, remove them to the platter. The onions
should be placed face side toward the heat for 3 to 5 minutes,
then rolled onto their sides to finish cooking, which will take
about 8 to 10 minutes. The onion skins will completely char.
When the onions are soft throughout, peel off the charred skins
and discard. Separate the onion layers, and set them on the platter, along with the other vegetables.

Preheat the oven to 350 degrees. To assemble, you may use
a large casserole for single-layering or a smaller but deeper casserole dish for a repeat layering of each vegetable. In either case,
make sure the dish is well oiled. Cover the bottom with the onion
slices, then the mushroom caps and stems, then the sliced pep-

pers, then the zucchini, then the eggplant, and finally the tomatoes. Sprinkle the tops of the tomatoes with the chopped basil leaves and the other minced herbs. Sprinkle a little salt and pepper, to taste, on the tomatoes and herbs. If using a small but deep casserole, repeat this layering with the remaining vegetables and herbs. Cover the casserole with a lid or foil. Bake for 30 minutes, which is just long enough to heat thoroughly and allow the flavors to blend.

Serve as either a side or main dish. Be sure to ladle the flavorful juice from the bottom of the casserole over the ratatouille as it is served.

SANDWICHES

Graduating from Hoagies

❧ Being a Philly boy I naturally have a strong bias for hoagies and cheesesteaks. Philadelphia was once known as the birthplace of liberty, a city rich in history. People in California seem to think of the city as the home of cheesesteaks and hoagies and the birthplace of the fictional Rocky Balboa, whose favorite eatery was Pat's Cheesesteaks. I would like to reverse that trend but, I am embarrassed to admit, whenever I go back to Philadelphia hoagies and cheesesteaks are higher on my to do list than the Liberty Bell and Independence Hall.

Hoagies, though, are no longer Philadelphia's prize possession. They have incarnated themselves all over the country under pseudonyms like grinders, heroes, and of course, submarine sandwiches—now, simply, subs. Philly boys, like me, are supposed to say and believe that none of these other versions is as good as a hoagie. I used to feel this way, actually, until recently. True, the myth of "the secret sauce" is a hoagie trademark, but it does not take a chemist to figure out that oil and spices sprinkled on a sandwich improve it. I never believed the urban legend that a hoagie must be made only on Philadelphia's famous Amoroso's hoagie rolls. Amoroso's bakery does make a great roll, perfect for the job but, really, not as unique as Philadelphians want to believe.

Like so much else in the world of food, sandwiches everywhere have been elevated to new levels of excellence. A hoagie, sub, or whatever you want to call it is a great sandwich when it is made with good ingredients and anybody's "secret sauce." I used to think that no other sandwich, except a cheesesteak, could satisfy me like a hoagie. Then I discovered good bread like Struan (a multi-grain bread described in great detail in *Brother Juniper's Bread Book*) and found some new combinations that, like hoagies, induce a particular kind of ecstasy.

The following sandwich ideas are included in this volume because they are easy to make and really good. I have seen some sandwich recipes in other books that look incredible, and I hope some day to make some of them, but often they depend on hard-to-find ingredients. The scarcest ingredient in these sandwiches is tasso, which is discussed in the chapter "Beyond Pasta." If you cannot find tasso (a good meat market should be able to order it for you), make your own substitute, using a good-quality ham and the spice blend described on page 149. Otherwise, the remaining ingredients are accessible and, when combined with the right bread, are a testament to the principles of symbiosis and synergy. The defining quality of a good sandwich, and the hoagie is undoubtedly the supreme archetype, is that the whole be greater than the sum of its parts.

The Right Bread

An often overlooked, yet vital principle in sandwich making is using the right bread. This will vary according to the sandwich. For instance, I am convinced that Struan or golden sesame bread, which are slightly sweet and moist, are the perfect breads for sandwiches like tuna or chicken salad. They do not work nearly as well with salami or sausage, for which I prefer grain of mustard seed, wild rice and onion, or roasted three-seed bread (recipes for these last two breads can be found in *Brother Juniper's Bread Book*). Some sandwiches are better on a soft French roll, some on grilled sliced bread, and some are great on either.

It would be ideal if you always made your own bread, but I think this is unrealistic, especially since wherever you live you should have access to good local bread and rolls; the bread revolution is sweeping the land. A hoagie or submarine roll should be fresh and fairly soft. Hard-crusted rolls can detract from a sandwich, competing rather than complementing. However, a fresh, crackly baguette makes a great sandwich bread—but only if it is fresh! Remember, a great sandwich begins with what bakers call "real bread."

Caveat

One other important note: Susan and I realize that we no longer live in Philadelphia when we order a submarine sandwich and they ask, "Mayo?" Perhaps, we now believe, the true distinction between a hoagie and a sub boils down to "secret sauce" versus mayo. ("Secret sauce" is the generic name used to describe the oil, vinegar, and spice blend that hoagie shops sprinkle over their sandwiches to make them, as they say, "Come alive.") Regardless, as the sandwiches below reveal, there is an appropriate time for mayo, as there is for secret sauce. We Philadelphians, as awakening members of the global community, are beginning to realize that not every great sandwich is a hoagie.

❧ Grilled Tasso and Cheese Sandwich

Susan and I used to make little sandwich kits to give as birthday gifts. We put all the ingredients for this in a carryout box, wrapped with a bow, and included assembly instructions. We knew the gift was a hit when the recipients brought up the subject a few weeks before their next birthday. They said things like, "Boy, that tasso sandwich kit was a great idea for a gift. Any chance you could . . . you know . . . ?" Here is how you can make your own.

For each sandwich you will need
2 ounces tasso, sliced paper thin (or tasso substitute, see
  page 149)
1 ounce (2 slices) provolone cheese, thinly sliced
4 marinated sun-dried tomatoes, or 2 slices fresh tomato
3–4 peperoncini (pickled peppers), split and spread open
Sliced onion, to taste
2 slices whole grain or rye bread
½ tablespoon mayonnaise
1 teaspoon Dijon, or sweet and hot mustard (your choice)
1 tablespoon softened butter or margarine

Assemble the sandwich fixings, making sure the meat and cheese are sliced as thin as possible. On one slice of bread spread mayonnaise and on the other spread the mustard. Build the sandwich on the mustard side, beginning with the tasso, then cheese, then tomatoes, peperoncini, and onion. Top with the second slice. On the outside of each slice of bread spread the butter or margarine and grill in a medium-hot skillet as you would a grilled cheese sandwich (see Note). When the first side is perfectly toasted to a golden brown, flip the sandwich and toast the other side. It will take about 2 or 3 minutes on each side. The cheese should melt at the same time the bread is toasting.

NOTE: Two tricks for grilling sandwiches: Place a weight on the sandwich, or steadily press down with a metal spatula to promote even toasting; or you may cover the skillet with a lid to keep the heat in, causing the cheese to melt faster.

Curried Chicken Salad Sandwich

SERVES 4 TO 6

During certain times of the year Susan and I go through curry cravings. Sometimes we get them during the winter rainy season, impelling us toward the kitchen to make pots of curried rice and vegetable stews. During the warmer seasons we tend to crave cold curry such as the following chicken salad sandwich.

Commercial curry spice, depending on the brand, can include cumin, coriander, turmeric, cayenne, cardamom, ginger, fenugreek, cinnamon, garlic, cloves, mustard, black pepper, and salt. If you are a hard-core curry fanatic, you probably prefer to make your own blend, toasting the spices in a dry skillet to bring out the flavors and sending an intoxicating aroma throughout your home. I find the spices to be both stimulating and comforting, another mysterious paradox from the world of food.

This chicken curry can be made with or without the skin cracklings. It is important, however, to roast the chicken with the skin on to ensure moistness. The addition of the cracklings adds a bacon-like flavor to the curry. There is enough chicken salad in this recipe to make up to 6 regular sandwiches.

1 whole roasting chicken, about 4 pounds
1 teaspoon freshly ground black pepper
1 tablespoon granulated garlic
¾ cup mayonnaise
½ cup fresh lemon juice
2 tablespoons curry powder
1 medium red onion, diced
2 small apples, finely chopped
⅓ cup raisins
½ teaspoon salt
Sandwich accessories: bread, mayonnaise, lettuce, apple, sweet
    onion, and *jicama*

Preheat the oven to 450 degrees (400 degrees if using a convection oven). Remove the giblet and neck from the chicken and rinse the chicken off under cold water. Combine the black pepper and granulated garlic and spread it all over the outside of the chicken. Place the chicken, breast side down, in a roasting pan and place in the oven. Immediately reduce the heat to 350 degrees (300 degrees in a convection oven). Bake for 1 hour, then turn the chicken breast-side up and bake for ½ hour more, or until completely cooked; the wings should pull off easily when done. Remove from the oven and let cool for at least 30 minutes.

When cool enough to handle, remove the skin. You may either discard it, save it for soup stock, or use it in the curry. If using in the curry, return the skin to the oven for about 20 minutes, or until it crisps like bacon. Remove it from the oven and chop into small pieces.

Remove all the meat from the chicken, saving the carcass for soup stock (see page 113). Chop the meat into bite-size pieces and place in a mixing bowl. Add all the remaining ingredients except the sandwich accessories, mixing thoroughly. If using the skin cracklings, add them last. Refrigerate the salad for 30 minutes to allow the flavors to blend.

Make sandwiches on your favorite multi-grain bread, spreading a little mayonnaise on the bread, adding a layer of lettuce, the curried chicken salad, thinly sliced apple, and a slice of sweet onion such as Walla Walla or Vidalia, or use red onion. You may also use a slice of peeled *jicama,* a crunchy and refreshing root vegetable that tastes like a cross between a radish and water chestnut and is as sweet as an apple. This sandwich can also be made on a hoagie roll or fresh baguette.

ह Roasted Garlic and Grilled Vegetable Sandwich

It is hard to believe that a mere ten years ago the idea of roasted garlic was practically unknown except by a few Chez Panisse culinary pilgrims. Since then, roasted garlic has become de rigueur, *often served as a butter replacement or a side dish in both trendy and neighborhood restaurants.*

As described below, there are a number of ways to roast garlic. At home we go through it at such an enormous rate that we keep a supply of roasted garlic cloves in both the refrigerator and the freezer. It is like having a secret ingredient that you can pull out at any time to add a touch of complexity to otherwise simple dishes. The combination of roasted garlic and the flavors of fire-roasted sweet peppers and other grilled vegetables in this rich vegetable sandwich make it one of the most satisfying imaginable.

Roasting the Garlic

Garlic can be roasted either in the skin or out. The easiest way is to roast the entire unpeeled head till the softened cloves are like butter in paper. Another way, especially if you need a large quantity, is to peel the cloves in advance, or buy a jar of peeled fresh garlic. This is becoming more widely available—we usually buy a three-pound jar and roast all of it. Here are the methods:

WHOLE GARLIC ROASTING METHODS

Method 1—Preheat the oven to 250 degrees. Rub a little olive oil on the outside of each head of unpeeled garlic. A faster method, if you are roasting a number of heads, is to pour a few tablespoons of olive oil in the casserole and roll the garlic heads in it. Roast as many heads as you like. Place them in the casserole root side down. Cover the dish and roast for 1 hour. Then turn the heads root side up and roast an additional hour, or until the heads are soft and the garlic pulp squeezes out easily from the skin. Save the garlic-infused oil in the casserole for cooking or for flavoring other dishes.

Method 2—Follow the same method as above, baking at 350 degrees for 1 hour, turning the heads after 30 minutes. The stem side of the garlic will slightly caramelize in the oil, which adds a nice flavor to the oil and to the garlic. Finish roasting the garlic on a charcoal or lava grill for approximately 10 minutes.

Method 3—Simply place whole heads of garlic, not oiled, in the oven directly on the oven rack, and bake at 350 degrees for about 1 hour, or until soft.

INDIVIDUAL GARLIC CLOVE METHOD

Preheat the oven to 350 degrees. Place the peeled cloves in a bowl and add just enough olive oil to coat them. Toss until all are covered. Transfer the cloves to a baking sheet and bake for about

45 minutes, or until all are soft and beginning to caramelize. You will need to stir them two or three times while they roast for even cooking. Remove from the oven and store the garlic cloves in freezer bags, refrigerating those that will be used within one or two days and freezing the remainder.

Grilling the Vegetables

Refer to the chapter on Ratatouille (page 157). Any of the vegetables in that dish work well in this sandwich. However, the most important are the sweet red peppers. Whenever we are grilling peppers, we always make more than we need because they are so versatile and keep well, either refrigerated or frozen. Marinate and grill the vegetables according to the instructions on page 160. For this sandwich, in addition to the sweet peppers, you may use mushrooms, zucchini, eggplant, onions, and even tomatoes.

The Sandwich

Served on freshly baked French bread, this is a wonderful baguette sandwich. In addition to a supply of roasted garlic and grilled vegetables you will need only a splash of "secret sauce" (page 175), to bring out the flavors, and fresh basil leaves, if available.

Cut the baguettes into the desired lengths and slice them open, leaving them slightly hinged. Spread the roasted garlic on the inside of the bread, like butter, and build your sandwich with the grilled sweet peppers, other vegetables, and the fresh basil. Splash the "secret sauce" over the vegetables, close the sandwich, and enjoy!

You can also serve this sandwich hot. See Grinder instructions on page 177.

❧ Refreshing Vegetable Sandwich

*This is a surprisingly simple and delicious sandwich. I like it,
especially, because of the* jìcama, *which is sweet, crisp, and cool.
As in the Roasted Garlic and Grilled Vegetable Sandwich, the
roasted red peppers are a critically important ingredient. We always make this sandwich on Struan bread, but if you cannot get
it, find the best multi-grain bread you can and give it a go.*

Struan or your favorite multi-grain bread
Mayonnaise (Best Foods or Hellmann's, or homemade)
Sunflower or alfalfa sprouts
Vine-ripened tomatoes, sliced
Grilled or roasted sweet red pepper (either commercial or
    homemade, page 160)
jìcama, thinly sliced
Sweet onion (such as Vidalia or Walla Walla), thinly sliced
Cucumber, peeled and sliced into rounds ¼ inch thick
Avocado slices (optional)
Coarsely ground fresh black pepper

To assemble the sandwiches, spread the mayonnaise on the
bread and then put on the sprouts and the tomato slices. Add the
remaining ingredients. You may omit either the onions or the
jìcama, but not both. Before closing the sandwich, sprinkle a
pinch of black pepper over all.

❧ California Hoagie

This is a more complex version of the Refreshing Vegetable Sand-

wich. I call it a California Hoagie because I still identify avocadoes with California foods, even though they have made their
way onto the menus of every state. Another reason is because
Japanese restaurants call sushi with avocado a California Roll, so
I am comforted in not being the only one to make this regionally
chauvinistic association (especially since Florida and Texas produce plenty of their own avocadoes—though not nearly as good
as the California Haas). Since moving to California, my latent
avocado tendencies have been fully actualized. Aside from guacamole, which runs rampant through this state in both wonderful and terrible renditions, my favorite use of avocado is pairing
it with fire-roasted (grilled) sweet peppers in this sandwich, a
hoagie in spirit if not fact. An excellent variation is made on
Struan or any multi-grain bread, then toasted in butter on a grill,
and served warm.

One final thought: There are some commercial peppermashes
that could be substituted for the Brother Juniper's version. They
are found in Asian food markets or the Oriental section of your
local supermarket under the generic name of Chile Garlic Sauce.

You will need the following ingredients:

Hoagie rolls (see Note) or sliced multi-grain bread
Sunflower or alfalfa sprouts (I prefer sunflower)
Ripe avocado, preferably Haas (a dark green medium
    California avocado), skinned and sliced into thin strips
Fresh onion strips
Vine-ripened tomato slices
Peperoncini (pickled peppers), split open so they will lay flat
Provolone cheese, thinly sliced (optional)
    "Secret Sauce" Dressing
½ cup red wine vinegar
½ cup light vegetable oil
¾ teaspoon salt

½ teaspoon freshly ground black pepper
½ teaspoon paprika
1 teaspoon dried oregano
2 tablespoons Brother Juniper's Chile Peppermash (page 6)

Assemble the sandwiches with the sprouts next to the bread. Use as much of each of the ingredients as your bread and taste will allow. When completely assembled, sprinkle the dressing over the entire filling, and close each sandwich.

NOTE: There is an old Philly trick regarding hoagie rolls. After you slice open the roll, scoop out some of the bread to make more room for the filling.

❧ Tuna Cheese Grinder

MAKES 3 GRINDERS

A grinder is a hot hoagie. The term first became popular in New England, where grinders are the Boston folk culture equivalent of a Philadelphia hoagie. I have to admit, which I can do without too much shame since I lived in Boston for six years, sometimes a grinder is more attractive than a hoagie. Almost any kind of hoagie, even the standard and supreme South Philadelphia Italian hoagie, can be turned into a tasty grinder by wrapping it in foil and baking it for ten minutes (or until the cheese melts). The following tuna cheese grinder relies on a great tuna salad served in classic grinder fashion.

Two 6⅛-ounce cans white tuna in water, drained
½ cup finely chopped onion
8 peperoncini (pickled peppers), stemmed and chopped

4 tablespoons fresh lemon juice

⅛ teaspoon freshly ground black pepper

2 tablespoons Brother Juniper's Chile Peppermash (page 6—also, see recipe introduction, page 175, for California Hoagie)

¾ cup mayonnaise

3 hoagie rolls or 1 French baguette

Sunflower sprouts

6 slices Provolone cheese

Preheat the oven to 400 degrees. Combine the first 7 ingredients and mix thoroughly. Slice the hoagie rolls or baguette and line with the sunflower sprouts. Fill the bread with tuna salad and then lay 2 slices of cheese over the tuna in each sandwich. If making one long baguette sandwich, use all the cheese. Wrap the sandwich(es) in aluminum foil and bake for 15 to 20 minutes.

TONICS

Putting Coke and Pepsi

Out of Business

❧ There was a time when sodas were called tonics and they were good for you. In principle, sodas should be health elixirs since they were originally made from herbs, spices, and other healthful ingredients. The original Dr. Pepper soda was basically carbonated prune juice. Coca-Cola was developed as an uplifting alternative to alcohol, an antidote to the psychological depression experienced by many Southerners after the Civil War (hence the cocaine extract in the original—not exactly a health drink, but coca had not yet revealed itself as the serpent's apple that we now know it to be). Sadly, it has been a while since root beer and ginger ale were good for us. The healing ingredients have long been replaced by artificial flavorings and huge amounts of sugar.

There has been an encouraging resurgence in the natural beverage industry the past few years, but total sales are a mere drop in the bucket compared to Coca-Cola and Pepsico. When we opened Brother Juniper's, I entertained fantasies (some would say delusions) of putting Coke and Pepsi out of business with natural sodas.

As a child I was a carbonation freak. Philadelphia was a great place to find real seltzer and good-tasting sodas like Frank's Black Cherry Wishniak, or Champ Cherry and Chocolate Soda made at the famous Levis Hot Dog store. You could still go into a soda fountain and get a birch beer or old-fashioned root beer on draft. Susan's grandmother actually worked as a nanny for the Hires family, of root beer fame.

I doubt that the sodas back then were any more healthful than today's commercial brands, but they left lasting impressions on my memory. Other people must feel the same way because there is a tremendous resurgence in the "old-fashioned" soda concept, with new brands and creative bottlings appearing all the time. Two enterprising local women have started a company called The Seltzer Sisters that features restored old-time glass seltzer spritzers, natural syrups, and chocolate egg cream mixes. The flavor industry has found new ways of making concentrated flavors, both natural and artificial, so it really is possible for anyone with a little marketing savvy to get into the soda business.

Ten years ago my ambitions were to revolutionize the industry by getting people excited about elixirs that were healthful. Why not substitute honey for sugar and freshly steeped herbs and spices in place of the ubiquitous artificial flavorings. This led me to create a number of home brews, mostly from ginger root and different herb and bark combinations. I am a confirmed believer in the tonic power of herbs, having consumed massive quantities of herbal concoctions while watching my various childhood allergies gradually disappear. I thought it possible for someone (me?) to become the Ben and Jerry, or Dr. Bronner anyway, of soda pop.

Since then I have seen a number of good natural sodas come and go. Many of them are made with ginger and ginseng. There are also some very good root beers on the market now. But I still believe, perhaps overoptimistically, that ginger fizz could have been one of the biggies. I am afraid, though, that Brother Juniper's Café took most of my entrepreneurial energy and I have passed the baton to others. Whether they can make the soda idea fly is still to be determined. It would give me great pleasure to be able one day to look back and say, "Yep, I gave Coke and Pepsi a good run for their money back then. Now everyone drinks ginger fizz and they don't even know where it began."

I can at least be content to know that we created a new word in the local vocabulary. Our customers never batted an eye when they proudly ordered a tall frosty mug of ginger fizz. We even got them to try an all-herbal tonic called "Forestville Fizz," one of the many names we gave it throughout the years.

It is fun and easy to make your own guilt-free and get-yourself-healthy sodas. The Coke and Pepsi empires may be safe for now but watch out you guys. If you can convince millions of people, as Coke so effectively has done, to want something that there is absolutely no real need for, consider the potential in offering something that is just as refreshing and may actually be good for you. It fills my heart with effervescence just thinking about it.

❧ Ginger Fizz Syrup

MAKES 3 DOZEN SODAS

11 cups water
1 pound unpeeled fresh ginger, sliced into ¼-inch-thick pieces
5½ cups honey
½ cup fresh-squeezed lemon juice, strained
½ cup fresh-squeezed lime juice, strained

Bring the water to a boil in a large pot. Toss in the sliced ginger, cover, and simmer for 15 minutes. Turn off the heat and add the honey. Allow to steep, uncovered, for 15 additional minutes. Stir and strain out the ginger. Add the lemon and lime juices. Let the syrup cool and store it in the refrigerator.

To make soda, fill a cold glass or frosted mug with 8 ounces of cold seltzer, club soda, or carbonated water. Add 4 ounces of cold Ginger Fizz Syrup and stir gently. You may add ice but it will weaken the carbonation.

Herbal Forestville Fizz Syrup

MAKES 3 DOZEN SODAS

11 cups water
11 Celestial Seasonings Red Zinger tea bags (or equivalent tea
  of any brand—the key is to get a blend with hibiscus and
  mint flavor)
5 cups honey
½ cup fresh-squeezed lemon juice, strained
½ cup fresh-squeezed lime juice, strained

Bring the water to a boil, turn off the heat, and add the tea bags. Cover and steep for 15 minutes. Remove the tea bags and add the honey, stirring until it dissolves. Add the lemon and lime juice and then transfer the mixture to a covered glass or plastic container and refrigerate.

To make soda, fill a cold glass or frosted mug with 8 ounces of cold seltzer, club soda, or carbonated water. Add 4 ounces of cold Forestville Fizz Syrup and stir gently.

NOTE: Both ginger and Forestville syrups may also be used in plain water as a refreshing noncarbonated drink, *à la* iced tea. Mixed with warm water, they make wonderful bedtime tonics. You may vary the proportion of syrup to water according to your taste.

Root Beer

MAKES 4 DOZEN SODAS

1 gallon water
¼ pound unpeeled fresh ginger, sliced into ¼-inch pieces
1 tablespoon wild cherry bark (available at many natural foods stores)
1 tablespoon vanilla extract
One 2-ounce bottle sarsaparilla extract concentrate (available at beer and wine-making supply houses)
8 cups honey

Bring the water to a boil. Add the ginger and simmer, covered, for 15 minutes. Turn off the heat and add the honey and wild cherry bark. Cover and steep 15 minutes. Strain out the cherry bark and ginger. Add the vanilla and sarsaparilla extract. Chill. Use the syrup as in Ginger Fizz: 4 ounces of syrup to 8 ounces of seltzer.

ઓ Vermont Elixir

One of the simplest and most effective tonics is made by mixing 2 teaspoons of honey and 1 tablespoon of unfiltered apple cider vinegar into 8 ounces of warm water. Drink throughout the day. According to folklore this drink will raise your resistance to colds and allergies. I am not allowed to make such claims, but I do believe them.

BREADS, MUFFINS,

&

SCONES

The Bread Book Revisited

❧ I learned a valuable lesson one day while preparing to make bread: Fatigue has a way of changing one's personality.

In the early days of Brother Juniper's Café, Susan and I had been putting in long days and were getting little sleep. We arrived about seven in the morning and began the prep work, which included baking the bread rolled out the night before. We attempted to open the doors by 11:00 A.M. for lunch, even without always having everything ready. Then the lunch rush hit, which lasted until about 2:00 P.M. We then had a few slow hours to replenish the soups and chilis, make fresh batches of whatever was needed, prepare more salad and dressings, brew the ginger fizz syrup, set up the bread doughs for the next day, and get ready for the dinner rush. The pressure was nearly unbearable. Some days, in the late afternoon, we often "hit the wall" and became, to be charitable, less than our usual exuberant selves. The key indicator was oversensitivity; anything at all became the hugest insult, setting off a chain reaction that ultimately led to upset and arguments between us.

We had just received some good reviews, including a front-page story in the daily paper, and were on the verge of a large surge in business. This meant more pressure. At four o'clock, an

hour before the anticipated onslaught, I went down to the base-
ment to bring up a fifty-pound sack of flour for the bread
doughs. On the way up the backstairs I must have nicked the
bag. As I passed the other shops in our building, walking quickly,
already muttering because of something that had happened during lunch, I heard the various shopkeepers call my name. "Yeah,
hi, hi," I said back, annoyed, and kept walking. As I entered the
café, intent on getting the sack off my shoulder, I saw Susan's
eyes open wide. She yelled, "Peter!"

Everyone in the café was laughing, which really made me angry. "What?!" I blurted, and turned around. There was a trail of
flour that looked like some sort of mole tunnel, winding out the
door, around the hall, and down the stairs. I groaned and Susan
started laughing again, which made me even angrier (what is it
about being laughed at that is so infuriating?). Suddenly each of
the shopkeepers appeared in the hallway with a vacuum-cleaner
and, as if choreographed for a vacuum-cleaner ballet, started
sweeping up the flour. Susan was still laughing. She said, "You
can laugh or cry but don't just stand there."

I actually did start to cry, feeling foolish, touchy, exhausted,
and frustrated. But then, with everyone else having such a good
time, I surrendered to the absurdity of the moment and joined in,
still feeling like a geek. Susan said, "These are the moments that
either make or break us—thank God we can still laugh."

"Yeah," I conceded.

That night we did over a thousand dollars in business, our first
thousand-dollar day. Susan was passing out complementary
glasses of ginger fizz in the hallway, assuring people they would
only have to wait fifteen more minutes for a table (we only had
six tables so all she could do was guess!).

The food held out, everyone was served, we survived, exhausted, and then faced an enormous cleanup. A few minutes
after closing there was the sound of band music out in the street,

growing closer and closer to the café. Suddenly, a group of musicians, brothers and sisters from our retreat center, marched in playing "When the Saints Go Marching In," and carrying a few bottles of champagne. After a brief celebration, they all stayed and helped us with the cleanup.

One of our customers told us that whenever he came to Brother Juniper's Café he felt like he was back in Berkeley. "Back in civilization," he called it. That night I felt like we were in New York City, though when we went home the blanket of stars in the sky above Forestville and the sounds of crickets and bullfrogs that replaced "When the Saints Go Marching In" made it clear we were still far from the madding crowds.

There were times ahead when it was not so easy to laugh, when the fatigue just engulfed us. During late nights, when one of us was on the verge of throwing in the towel, we learned to invoke the image of the vacuum-cleaner ballet on the day of the flour trail and the night of the marching saints. It helped, it helped.

In addition to learning about myself, I have learned a great deal more about bread since the publication of *Brother Junipers's Bread Book* in 1991. While promoting the book I was asked during many interviews, "What is it about bread that is so special?" In formulating a response I had a new insight and have been building my bread workshops and classes around it ever since. What sets bread apart from all other foods is the symbolism involved in the baking process. The baker takes three basic ingredients—flour, water, and salt—and forms a lump of dough, or clay. In addition, however, a spark of life, the leaven, is breathed into this lump. Leaven comes from root words meaning "to enliven, or vivify." Yeast is the leaven used in breads, and it transforms the lump into a living, breathing organism. The baker cultivates this dough by providing an environment for growth and by punching down the dough when it gets to a certain size. After the proper nurturing, the dough is shaped into a loaf and baked. At this time the yeast sacrifices its own life, dying when the temperature reaches 140 degrees. The raw dough is transformed into bread, which is then consumed, nourishing us. In no other culinary process does the craftsman so closely imitate the creativity of God, as described in Genesis.

I caution bread makers not to get too puffed up about this lofty description since making bread can be a humbling experience. The first French breads I ever baked in the oven at the café were a disaster. The thermostat was broken and the oven went up to what must have been 1,000 degrees. I put the breads in, not knowing, and returned in two minutes to spray them with water. The burst of heat and steam sent me reeling backwards. When I recovered, brushing off the remnants of my singed eyebrows, the bread had turned completely black. In two minutes! So much for the master craftsman. We promptly fixed the oven.

Though the general public seems to be been willing to settle for mediocre bread, a new trend toward traditional and neo-traditional breads has grown rapidly during the past few years. Happily, as good bakeries opened up all over the country, they have been supported with genuine joy and excitement; people are now discovering how good bread can be and are beginning to take a stand against mediocrity. There is a "bread revolution" taking place. Long live symbols!

This is a rather extensive introduction to some new breads and baked goods. It does, however, sum up what it took me almost two hundred pages to say in my previous book. What follows are some recipes that were developed after *Brother Juniper's Bread Book* was published.

In the unfolding of Brother Juniper's there has been an evolution of consciousness, reflected by our products. Bread has been, without doubt, my primary teacher these past few years. It has revealed me to myself and helped me to understand how life works. It has also been an extremely gruelling task master, unpredictable at times, though science claims to have tamed it (at the cost of creating inferior bread). Many other bakers have shared their lessons with me in order to help me develop what are now distinctively Brother Juniper's breads. Bakers are, by and large, a spiritual even if not overtly religious group. We have all been taught by the same master: a once lifeless lump of clay into which we have injected the breath of life, which then, in a final frenzy of oven spring, sacrificed itself on our behalf.

NOTE: All of the bread recipes both here and in *Brother Juniper's Bread Book* can be made in any model bread machine. You will need to divide the measurements proportionately to fit in your machine. One-pound machines generally take 2 cups of flour; one-and-a-half-pound machines require 3 cups. All other measurement changes are in direct ratio with the flour. If you find your loaves are not rising fully, you may need to adjust either the water (be sure your dough is soft and elastic, not stiff and dense), or increase the yeast in ½ teaspoon increments.

Some New Breads

Many of the following recipes call for milk or buttermilk. You may substitute water if you are one of the growing number of people moving into a vegan style of eating. Milk softens the crumb, so expect a tougher, nuttier texture if eliminating it.

These breads also call for high-gluten bread flour, which now can be found in most markets (often simply called "bread flour"). It is flour with a higher protein and gluten content, allowing for greater rising capacity. Unbleached all-purpose flour can be used, but it will yield a smaller loaf.

ਟੇ Cinnamon Raisin Struan

MAKES THREE 1 1/2-POUND LOAVES

Struan is the most popular bread we make. It is the ritual harvest bread of the Michaelmas Festival (Feast of St. Michael the Archangel), as once celebrated in western Scotland. It was the centerpiece recipe in Brother Juniper's Bread Book: Slowrise as Method and Metaphor. *After the book came out we discovered a way to make an exceptional raisin bread out of Struan. For this reason, I am going to repeat the recipe for Struan and add the instructions for turning it into cinnamon raisin bread.*

Struan, incidentally, aside from being the name of a Scottish clan, also means "the convergence of two or more streams." This seems to be a most appropriate name for a bread of such confluences, consisting of so many grains and ingredients. The addition of cinnamon and raisins adds yet another stream of influence to this already complex bread, but it also takes it to another level, making it my all-time favorite bread.

This recipe makes three 1½-pound loaves. It can be reduced in size, keeping all ingredients in proportion.

One important tip for this and all bread recipes: Because everyone measures ingredients differently, you should use the water measurement as a guideline, not an absolute. Add it last and always less than called for, being prepared to slowly add more as needed, even surpassing the amount called for if needed. The test is in the feel of the dough—it should be soft and elastic, tacky but not sticky. It should not be dense, dry, and easily rippable. When pulled, it should stretch like taffy, getting thin enough to almost see through. This is called window-paning.

7 cups high-gluten bread flour
½ cup uncooked polenta (coarse ground cornmeal)

½ cup rolled oats
½ cup brown sugar
⅓ cup wheat bran
4 teaspoons salt
2 tablespoons plus 1 teaspoon instant yeast or 3 tablespoons
  active dry yeast activated in 4 tablespoons lukewarm water
½ cup cooked brown rice
¼ cup honey
¾ cup buttermilk
About 1½ cups water (be prepared to add more if needed)
3 cups raisins
½ cup cinnamon sugar (1 part cinnamon to 2 parts granulated
  sugar)
4 tablespoons melted butter, margarine, or vegetable oil

In a large bowl, combine all the dry ingredients, including
the salt and yeast (unless using active dry yeast, which should be
activated in warm water and added with the wet ingredients).
Add the cooked rice, honey, and buttermilk and mix together.
Then add 1 cup of water, reserving the rest to add as needed.
With your hands, squeeze the ingredients together until they
make a ball. Sprinkle some flour on the counter and turn the ball
out of the bowl and begin kneading. Add small quantities of
water as needed.

Because Struan has so many whole grains, it takes longer to
knead than most breads. Allow at least 15 minutes, but be prepared to knead for 20. The dough will change before your eyes,
lightening in color, becoming gradually more elastic and evenly
grained. The finished dough should be tacky, not sticky, lightly
golden, stretchy and elastic, rather than porridge-like. When you
push the heels of your hands into the dough it should give way
but not tear. If it flakes or crumbles, add a little more water.

When the dough seems ready, add the raisins and knead for 2 more minutes, until the raisins are evenly distributed.

Wash out the mixing bowl and dry it thoroughly. Put in the dough and cover with a damp towel or plastic wrap, or place the bowl inside a plastic bag. Allow the dough to rise in a warm place for about 1 hour, until it has roughly doubled in size.

Cut the dough into 3 equal pieces (or more if you want to make smaller loaves). With a rolling pin, roll out each piece into a rectangle. Sprinkle about 1 tablespoon of cinnamon sugar over the surface, spreading it evenly. From the bottom of the long side, roll up the dough into tight loaves, tucking and pinching the seams into one line on the bottom. Put the loaves, seam side down, in greased bread pans (for full-sized loaves your pan should be around $9 \times 4\frac{1}{2} \times 3$ inches). Cover and allow the loaves to rise until doubled in size.

Preheat the oven to 350 degrees (300 degrees if using a convection oven). When the loaves have risen, cresting over the tops of the pans, place on the center shelf and bake for about 45 minutes. The loaves should be nicely domed and dark gold. The bottom and sides should be a uniform light gold and there should be an audible, hollow thwack when you tap the bottom of the loaf. If the loaves are not ready, remove them from the pans and place them back in the oven until done. They will bake quickly when removed from the pans.

When done, brush a little butter, margarine, or oil over the tops, then sprinkle with the remaining cinnamon sugar, coating each loaf with a layer of cinnamon crust.

Allow the breads to cool on wire racks for at least 40 minutes before slicing. This bread makes exceptional breakfast toast and French toast!

‹❧ Grain of Mustard Seed Bread

MAKES 3 LOAVES, 4 BAGUETTES OR
BÂTARDS, OR 3 DOZEN DINNER ROLLS

The idea for this bread came from a true story told by Dr. Nor-
man Vincent Peale in which a man turned his life around by
carrying a grain of mustard seed in his pocket to remind him
how much (or little) faith was required in order to move moun-
tains. In order to keep from losing his mustard seed he had it
embedded in plastic. As a result of this reminder he came up with
an idea for mustard seed jewelry and ornaments, which allowed
him to start his own business, support his family, and get a new
lease on life.

The mustard seeds add a spicy pop-in-your-mouth quality to
this bread, which goes well with salmon and other seafood, espe-
cially when you add the dill. This is a good bread to serve at
Sunday brunches with smoked fish platters. You may also turn it
into rolls and serve them at elegant dinners. The mustard finish
complements fine food and wine; I would not recommend it with
peanut butter and jelly.

8 cups high-gluten bread flour
½ cup wheat bran
2 tablespoons instant yeast or 2½ tablespoons active dry yeast
    activated in 4 tablespoons lukewarm water
2 tablespoons dried dill (optional)
1 tablespoon salt
½ cup whole mustard seeds soaked overnight in 1 cup water
½ cup buttermilk
½ cup honey (or sugar)
About 1½ cups water

In a large bowl, combine all the dry ingredients. Add the mustard seeds, including the soaking water, and the remaining ingredients, reserving a little water for adjustments during kneading. Turn the dough onto a floured counter and knead for 10 to 15 minutes. The dough should be elastic, soft, and tacky, but not sticky. Return the dough to a clean bowl and cover with plastic wrap or a damp towel, or put the bowl inside a plastic bag. Allow the dough to rise in a warm place for about 1 hour, or until doubled in size.

The dough can be baked in loaf pans, be baked free form on baking pans, or be shaped into rolls.

Dinner rolls are usually about 2 ounces (unbaked), or the size of a Ping-Pong ball. They can be formed by rolling the pieces of dough on a dry surface under the palm of your hand, cupping it to provide shaping and pressure. Bake on a very lightly greased baking pan, allowing 3 inches between rolls (or cluster them in interesting combinations for pull-apart rolls).

Baguettes and *bâtards* (shorter, stubby submarine-shaped 1-pound loaves) are formed by rolling out the dough to the desired length (18 to 24 inches for a baguette, 12 inches for a *bâtard*), and rolling it up into a cigar or submarine shape, carefully pinching the seam closed. Always remember to keep the seam on the bottom. Make the loaves tight, with lots of surface tension, to hold the shape during rising and baking. Sprinkle a strip of polenta or coarse cornmeal on the pan and put the dough on it to give a crunchy bottom crust.

A loaf bread should half-fill the pan. Make sure the pan is evenly greased. When the dough rises, it will crest over the top, doming, which is when it should be baked. By baking it while still on the rise you should get about a 10–15 percent oven spring in the finished loaf. If you wait until the dough is fully risen, it often will fall in the oven, or spread to the sides.

In all cases, cover and allow the loaves to double in size.

Baguettes and *bâtards* should be slashed with a razor or serrated knife just before baking to ensure even baking and an attractive presentation. Make the slashes about ¾ of an inch deep, angled rather than straight down, cutting on a slight diagonal down the length of the loaf. Make 4 slashes for a baguette, 3 for a *bâtard*.

Bake baguettes and *bâtards* in a preheated 425-degree oven (375 degrees if using a convection oven), spraying with water at 2-minute intervals during the first 6 minutes. This will give a nice crust, approximating the steam ovens used in professional bakeries.

Pan breads and rolls should be baked at 350 degrees (300 degrees if using a convection oven). Rolls take about 20 minutes; loaves 45 to 60 minutes, depending on size. See instructions for Cinnamon Raisin Struan (page 196) for determining doneness.

❧ Volcano Bread

MAKES 1 LOAF

This is a fun bread, a variation of stromboli *(stuffed bread),* focaccia, *and pizza. It is great for parties or sporting events, and kids really love it.*

1 pound any kind of bread dough, preferably basic French bread
2 cups grated cheese (Cheddar, Swiss, jack, mozzarella, or a mixture)
2 cups any combination of diced onion, diced red bell peppers, roasted garlic, sliced green or black olives, mung bean sprouts, or your favorite pizza toppings

If using basic French bread dough, allow it to rise twice. For any other doughs, allow them to rise only once. Then, divide the dough into 16 equal pieces. Roll them into little balls. Place 8 pieces in a greased 9-inch loaf pan. Sprinkle half the cheese and vegetable mixture over the dough. Put the remaining 8 dough pieces on top and spread the remaining cheese and vegetables over the top of it.

Cover and allow to rise for 45 minutes, or until the bread is near, but not over, the top of the pan. Place in a preheated 350 degree oven (300 degrees if using a convection oven). Your oven will stay cleaner if you put the loaf pan on a sheet pan to catch drips. Bake until the cheese turns a deep golden color, about 1 hour. Remove the bread from the oven and, using a knife or pastry blade, go around the edges of the bread to loosen it from the pan. Quickly flip the bread out of the pan, resting it upside down on the sheet pan. Allow it to cool for 10 minutes, then move it to a cooling rack, right side up.

This is a pull-apart bread, which means the pieces will come off with a gentle tug. Pass it around as you would a bowl of popcorn, or serve at the table in place of rolls.

❧ Honey Jalapeño Bread

MAKES 3 LOAVES, 4 BAGUETTES OR
BÂTARDS, OR 3 DOZEN DINNER ROLLS
This is a sweet and hot bread, different from the Cajun Three-Pepper Bread described in Brother Juniper's Bread Book. *I have become very fond of the sweet/hot flavor combination, which is very prominent in Oriental cuisines. The sweetness serves as a*

flavor intensifier for the hot spices and gives the bread a long finish.

8 cups high-gluten bread flour
2 cups sliced fresh jalapeño peppers or commercial jalapeño "nacho rings" (sliced pickled jalapeño peppers)
½ cup wheat bran
1 cup honey
½ cup buttermilk
3 tablespoons instant yeast or 4 tablespoons active dry yeast activated in 4 tablespoons lukewarm water
1 tablespoon salt
2 tablespoons vinegar or 2 tablespoons commercial "nacho ring" liquid
About 1¾ cups water

This recipe follows the same basic steps of mixing, shaping, and baking as Grain of Mustard Seed Bread. Please refer to pages 198–199 for step-by-step instructions.

ꙮ Golden Sesame Bread

MAKES 3 LOAVES, 4 BAGUETTES OR
BÂTARDS, OR 3 DOZEN DINNER ROLLS
This is the most popular new bread we have developed in the past three years. It captures a Middle Eastern quality, evoking memories of one of my favorite confections, halvah. The flavors are so pleasant that this bread can be used with almost any food, from the simple to the complex. I find that it complements poultry dishes especially well, but have also enjoyed it with tuna, peanut

butter and jelly, and meats of various kinds. It is also one of those breads that I often eat all by itself, with nothing on it. I have been known to eat a whole loaf while en route from the bakery to my home, and then suggesting to Susan that we skip dinner since, "I'm not very hungry." I think she has figured out the cause.

8 cups high-gluten bread flour
2 cups sesame seeds (raw, not blanched)
½ cup wheat bran
1 cup honey
½ cup buttermilk
1 tablespoon salt
3 tablespoons instant yeast or 4 tablespoons active dry yeast
    activated in 4 tablespoons lukewarm water
About 1¾ cups water

This recipe follows the same basic steps of mixing, shaping, and baking as Grain of Mustard Seed Bread. Please refer to pages 198–199 for step-by-step instructions.

🐦 Pumpkin Spice Bread

MAKES 3 LOAVES, 4 BAGUETTES OR
BÂTARDS, OR 3 DOZEN DINNER ROLLS

We received great compliments for this bread, which was developed to fill a special request by a local hotel for a Thanksgiving roll.

8 cups high-gluten bread flour
½ cup wheat bran

1 tablespoon cinnamon
1 teaspoon powdered ginger
1 teaspoon powdered allspice
½ teaspoon grated nutmeg
1 cup sugar
1 cup pumpkin purée
1 tablespoon salt
About 2 cups buttermilk
2 tablespoons instant yeast or 2½ tablespoons active dry yeast
  activated in 4 tablespoons lukewarm water

This recipe follows the same basic steps of mixing, shaping, and baking as Grain of Mustard Seed Bread. Please refer to pages 198–199 for step-by-step instructions.

⁊ Orange Cranberry Bread

MAKES 3 LOAVES, 4 BAGUETTES OR
BÂTARDS, OR 3 DOZEN DINNER ROLLS

The same hotel that had asked for a Thanksgiving bread asked for another special bread for Christmas (some of our best ideas come as a result of special requests), so we came up with this one. Not only was the hotel chef thrilled but most of our staff gobbled up the extras. I have to admit, this recipe makes one of the most delightful dinner rolls I have ever had, and it is not necessary to wait until Christmas to make it.

8 cups high-gluten bread flour
½ cup wheat bran
1 cup sugar

1 tablespoon salt
3 tablespoons instant yeast or 4 tablespoons active dry yeast
    activated in 4 tablespoons lukewarm water
1 cup buttermilk
½ cup orange juice concentrate
About 1¼ cups water
2 cups cranberries

This recipe follows the same basic steps of mixing, shaping, and baking as Grain of Mustard Seed Bread. Please refer to pages 198–199 for step-by-step instructions. Wait to add the cranberries until the final 2 minutes of kneading. The berries will break and add a little moisture to the dough. If necessary, sprinkle a little extra flour on the counter if the dough shows signs of becoming sticky.

❧ Hot Cross Buns

MAKES 3 DOZEN
This is an original version of an Easter favorite. Hot cross buns are traditionally served on Palm Sunday to celebrate what is known as "the triumphant entry of Jesus into Jerusalem."

8 cups high-gluten bread flour
½ cup wheat bran
1 cup sugar
1 tablespoon salt
2 tablespoons instant yeast or 2½ tablespoons active dry yeast
    activated in 4 tablespoons lukewarm water
1 cup buttermilk

½ cup orange juice concentrate
About 1¼ cups water
2 cups currants
   Glaze
1 cup powdered sugar
½ cup water

Follow the basic instructions for making Grain of Mustard Seed Bread (see pages 198–199).

When the dough has completed its first rise, divide it into 36 equal pieces. Form them into individual rolls by cupping the palms of your hands and, using downward pressure, round the pieces between your hands and the table (with a little practice you will be able to round one in each hand simultaneously). Place 12 roll pieces on each of 3 lightly greased baking sheets, spacing the rolls about 2 inches apart. Cover the baking sheets with a clean tea towel or with plastic wrap (or do as I do, and slip each pan into a clean plastic bag). Set in a slightly warm place to rise for about 60 to 90 minutes, or until the rolls are double in size.

Preheat the oven to 350 degrees, or 300 degrees if using a convection oven. With a sharp serrated knife, cut a small cross in the top of each roll, about ¼-inch deep, and then place all three pans in the oven to bake. Rotate the pans every 6 minutes, so that each pan bakes on all three oven shelves. The rolls should take about 20 or 25 minutes to bake. They will be firm and hollow sounding when thumped on the bottom, and the crust should be a light golden brown.

Make the glaze: Stir the ingredients together until the sugar is dissolved, forming a thick paste.

After the rolls have cooled for 15 minutes, fill in the cross marks with the glaze, using a knife or spoon.

Let the rolls cool for another 15 minutes before eating or serving them.

❧ Rosemary Stuffing Bread

MAKES 3 LOAVES, 4 BAGUETTES OR BÂTARDS, OR 3 DOZEN DINNER ROLLS

There is a large hedge of rosemary bushes growing outside the original Brother Juniper's facility in Forestville. I go there every Christmas, Easter, and Thanksgiving to harvest enough rosemary to get us through the holiday season.

This bread can be used for stuffing, for which it was created, but it also makes a delicious and unusual loaf or dinner roll and is especially good with poultry or lamb. If you are planning to use it this way, omit the sage, so that the flavor of the rosemary is clear and strong.

To use the bread for stuffing, cut up the finished loaves to crouton size, and dry the pieces overnight in an oven set on its lowest temperature. Since the flavoring is already in the bread, you need only add whatever special ingredients are in your favorite recipe and voilà! Or you can try the colorful harvest stuffing, which follows on page 207.

8 cups high-gluten bread flour
½ cup wheat bran
1 cup cooked wild rice or wild and brown rice blend
1 cup diced fresh onion or ⅓ cup chopped dried onions
⅓ cup brown sugar
½ cup buttermilk

2 tablespoons instant yeast or 2½ tablespoons active dry yeast
   activated in 4 tablespoons lukewarm water
1½ tablespoons powdered sage (see Note)
2 tablespoons fresh rosemary or 1 tablespoon powdered dry
   rosemary (see Note)
½ tablespoon powdered thyme (see Note)
2 tablespoons dried parsley or 4 tablespoons minced fresh
   parsley
About 1¾ cups water

This recipe follows the same basic steps of mixing, shaping, and baking as Grain of Mustard Seed Bread. Please refer to pages 198–199 for step-by-step instructions.

NOTE: Powdered herbs can usually be found next to the whole dried herbs in most markets. If you cannot find powdered herbs, powder whole herbs in a dry blender.

૨૦ Savory Harvest Stuffing

SERVES 4 TO 6

8 cups dried and crumbled or cubed Rosemary Stuffing Bread
   (1 large loaf)
1 cup coarsely chopped walnuts
1 cup diced onion
1 cup diced celery
4 cups chicken broth
1 pound diced sausage, such as andouille, chaurice (creole),
   chorizo, or other spicy sausage, pan-fried until crisp
   (optional)

Salt and freshly ground black pepper to taste
   Topping
1 tablespoon vegetable oil
1 large sweet red bell pepper, sliced into thin strips
1 medium onion, sliced into thin strips
1 cup thinly sliced fresh mushrooms

Mix together all the ingredients except the topping. Adjust the salt and pepper. Stuff the bird (turkey or chicken) and roast. Or bake the stuffing in a greased, covered casserole dish in a preheated 350 degree oven for 1 hour.

Ten minutes before serving, prepare the topping: Heat a frying pan with the oil and sauté the pepper, onion, and mushrooms until the onion is translucent and the pepper strips are shiny and still bright red. Remove the vegetables from the pan with a slotted spoon, leaving the pan juices behind. (Save the juices for a soup stock.)

When serving, spread the onion, pepper, and mushroom topping over the stuffing for a colorful presentation.

ஃ Lemon Rice Bread with Dill

MAKES 3 LOAVES, 4 BAGUETTES OR
BÂTARDS, OR 3 DOZEN DINNER ROLLS

I am very excited about this new bread. It has a great crust and texture, and a delicious tart finish. Made without dairy or sweeteners, the dough should be treated like French bread, which means three rises instead of two.

8 cups high-gluten bread flour

4 cups cooked rice (you may substitute any cooked grain, including wild rice, quinoa, bulgur, millet, or oats)

4 tablespoons chopped fresh dill (optional)

2 tablespoons instant yeast or 2½ tablespoons active dry yeast activated in 4 tablespoons lukewarm water

1½ tablespoons salt

2 cups fresh lemon juice

Water as needed (determined by how wet the cooked grain is)

This recipe follows the same basic steps of mixing, shaping, and baking as Grain of Mustard Seed Bread. Please refer to pages 198–199 for step-by-step instructions, with the following addition:

After the first rise, knead the dough back to its original size (also called "punching down" the dough). Form it into a ball again and allow it to rise one more time in the bowl, about 1 hour. After the second rise, proceed to form the loaves as instructed and allow them to rise a third time.

The extra rise allows this dough to develop more character, as with French and sourdough breads. Because no sugar or dairy is added, the dough can sustain the extra rise without exhausting the yeast.

New Muffins

The most important criterion for our muffins is that they be moist, not dry. They must also impress with bold flavor. The following muffin recipes are ones I have developed since the publication of Brother Juniper's Bread Book. *Each recipe makes 12 very large muffins. You may save unbaked muffin batter in the refrigerator for up to 5 days, or freeze it for up to 1 month.*

❧ Lemon Walnut Muffins

MAKES 12 LARGE MUFFINS

Dry ingredients
4 cups sifted unbleached all-purpose flour
1 teaspoon salt
1 teaspoon baking soda
1½ teaspoons baking powder
1½ cups white sugar
2 cups walnuts, coarsely chopped (or broken pieces)
Wet ingredients
2 large eggs, slightly beaten
½ cup canola or vegetable oil
1 cup fresh lemon juice
2 cups buttermilk
1½ teaspoons lemon extract

Sift the dry ingredients together. In another bowl, combine the wet ingredients and beat until the mixture is smooth. Mix the wet and dry ingredients together only until the flour disappears. In a greased muffin pan (you may use muffin papers in the muffin pan, but you still need to grease the pan), fill the cups to slightly above the rim. Place the muffin pan on a baking sheet to catch any drips.

Preheat the oven to 350 degrees, or 300 degrees if using a convection oven. Bake the muffins for about 35 minutes on the middle shelf. When done they will be golden on top and springy when pressed in the center. (You can also test them by sticking a toothpick into the center. If it comes out clean then the muffins are done.) Remove them from the oven but let them rest in the pan for at least 20 minutes to set. You may then remove them from the pan. As with bread, the muffins are still cooking as they cool. They are best eaten 1 hour after baking.

૨ Honey Almond Muffins

MAKES 12 LARGE MUFFINS

Dry ingredients
4 cups unbleached all-purpose flour
1 teaspoon salt
1 teaspoon baking soda
1½ teaspoons baking powder
2 cups slivered almonds, toasted in the oven
Wet ingredients
2 large eggs, slightly beaten
½ cup canola or vegetable oil
2 cups buttermilk
1½ cups honey
1½ teaspoons almond extract

Follow the directions for making the batter and baking Lemon Walnut Muffins (see page 210).

૨ Maple Walnut Muffins

MAKES 12 LARGE MUFFINS

Dry ingredients
4 cups unbleached all-purpose flour
1 teaspoon salt

1 teaspoon baking soda
1½ teaspoons baking powder
2 cups walnuts, coarsely chopped (or broken pieces)
    Wet ingredients
2 large eggs, slightly beaten
½ cup canola or vegetable oil
1¾ cups pure maple syrup (or maple-flavored pancake syrup)
1½ cups buttermilk
1½ teaspoons maple or vanilla extract

Follow the directions for making the batter and baking Lemon Walnut Muffins (see page 210).

🐜 Pumpkin Muffins

MAKES 12 LARGE MUFFINS

Dry ingredients
4 cups unbleached all-purpose flour
1 teaspoon salt
1 teaspoon baking soda
1½ teaspoons baking powder
1½ cups white sugar
1½ teaspoons cinnamon
½ teaspoon powdered ginger
½ teaspoon powdered allspice
¼ teaspoon grated nutmeg
    Wet ingredients
2 large eggs, slightly beaten
1¼ cups pumpkin purée or canned pumpkin (a 16-ounce can)

2½ cups buttermilk
¾ cup canola or vegetable oil
1½ teaspoons vanilla extract

Follow the directions for making the batter and baking Lemon Walnut Muffins (see page 210).

🥨 Sal's Scones

MAKES 12

Salvador Ceja is our chief dough maker. He is also a creative chef and product developer. He has won a number of chili and pot roast competitions and, if there is ever a scone contest, I feel certain that this recipe would win. A scone is nothing more than a sweet tea biscuit, but it is astounding how many mediocre, dry scones are sold every day in coffee houses. I was about to swear off them for good when Sal made some as a Christmas gift for the staff. They were so much better than any scones I had ever had, even in England and Scotland, I asked him if he would add them to the bakery's repertoire. With Sal's permission, here is his scone formula—cherish it!

3 cups all-purpose flour
½ cup sugar
1 tablespoon baking powder
½ teaspoon baking soda
⅛ teaspoon salt
2 teaspoons grated fresh lemon zest
1 cup currants
¼ pound butter

½ cup light vegetable oil (canola, safflower, or soy)
1 cup buttermilk
1 large egg, slightly beaten
¼ cup fresh lemon juice
1 egg, well beaten, for egg wash

Preheat the oven to 350 degrees (300 degrees if using a convection oven). In a bowl, mix together all the dry ingredients, including the lemon zest and currants. Make a well in the center of this mixture.

In a saucepan, melt the butter and add the vegetable oil. Cool until only slightly warm.

Combine the butter/oil mixture with the buttermilk, beaten egg, and the lemon juice, whisking until well mixed. Add this mixture to the dry ingredients, pouring it into the well and working quickly with your hands or a large spoon to mix it into a dough. Do not overmix, as this will toughen the dough.

Form into a round, flat loaf, about 2-inches thick. Cut the loaf into 12 wedges and place them on a lightly greased baking sheet, allowing 1 inch between pieces. Another option is to roll out the loaf 1 inch thick and cut out rounds with a biscuit cutter or drinking glass. Though this is not how Sal does it, the rounds are a more familiar scone shape; I prefer the wedges. Brush each scone with some of the beaten egg. You may freeze unbaked scones and bake them later.

Bake for about 25 minutes, or until the scones turn golden brown on top and bottom. Cool on a rack for at least 15 minutes before eating.

A FEW DESSERTS

The Chocolate Queen

Reigneth

  Susan and I are both chocoholics. She often proudly wears a sweatshirt that says, "OK, give me some chocolate and nobody gets hurt." As the cook at our retreat center she was responsible for birthdays and celebrations and used those times to try out new chocolate desserts. She soon became known as the Chocolate Queen. Some of the more mystically inclined whispered that she had a chocolate aura. All I know is she made some outrageously delectable creations.

Chocolate is so good in and of itself that sometimes the best thing to do with it is practice the "KISS" method (keep it simple, stupid). Susan's brownies, for example, are hard to beat even by the new wave of chocolate "decadence" desserts on the market. The best thing to do with chocolate is to showcase it.

I returned to my hometown, Philadelphia, a few years ago as guest chef at LeBus Restaurant for the annual Book and the Cook event. The menu that owner/chef David Braverman planned included Susan's brownies. I made them the night before the event, taking care to "properly underbake" them (see recipe to follow). The pans were larger than we use at our bakery so I miscalculated and actually underbaked a little too much. The center of the pan contained a chocolate ooze that was, I

must admit, unbelievably delicious, even if not, technically, a
brownie. The serving staff held back some of this for themselves.
As I was making my way to the dining room to greet the customers, many of whom were childhood friends and relatives ex-
periencing Brother Juniper's food for the first time, one of the
waiters stopped me and asked, "Did you make those brownies?"
I admitted yes and then he said, "I want you to know that those
brownies were so good that, that . . . that they're better than
sex!" He then added, "And I ought to know, because I've had
sex."

His colleague, standing nearby, said, "If you think any brownies are better than sex, then you've never had sex."

The waiter replied, "Then you've never tried these brownies.
In fact, the only thing better than these brownies is brownies and
sex!"

My reply could only be, "Gee, thanks, but I'm too close to the
subject to make a call." Thus does the Chocolate Queen reign
over all.

❧ The World's Greatest Brownies

MAKES 16 LARGE (2-INCH) OR 32 SMALL
(1-INCH) BROWNIES

Brownie
1¼ cups all-purpose flour
2 cups white sugar
1 teaspoon baking powder
1 teaspoon salt
½ pound plus 2 tablespoons butter

4 ounces unsweetened baking chocolate (Be sure to use a good-quality chocolate such as Ghirardelli. It really does make a difference.)

1 teaspoon vanilla extract

4 large eggs, beaten until frothy

1 cup chopped walnuts or pecans

Frosting

½ cup boiling water (You may not need all of it.)

2 cups powdered sugar

¼ pound butter

4 ounces unsweetened baking chocolate

½ teaspoon vanilla extract

Preheat the oven to 350 degrees (300 degrees if using a convection oven). In a bowl, combine all the dry ingredients, except the nuts.

Melt the butter in a saucepan large enough to also hold the chocolate. When the butter is melted, turn down the heat and immediately add the chocolate. Remove the pan from the heat and stir until both the chocolate and the butter are completely incorporated. Add the vanilla and then the eggs. Whisk until mixed.

Add the wet mixture to the dry and whisk until smooth and creamy. Stir in the nuts. (Do not mix the nuts with the dry ingredients because the flour will get trapped in the nutmeats and make white spots in the batter.)

Pour the batter into a greased 6 × 9-inch or 8 × 8-inch pan (or line a greased pan with waxed paper) and bake for 22 minutes; check. It may take as long as 30 minutes, depending on the oven. The brownie is done when the edges are firm but the very center jiggles slightly when shaken. If you wait until the center is firm the brownie will be more cakelike and less fudgy.

Remove from the oven and allow the brownie to cool completely, in the pan. You can frost the brownie in the pan or remove it from the pan (if you used waxed paper) to frost. I prefer to invert the brownie and frost the bottom, which is nice and flat. This necessitates using the waxed-paper method.

To frost the brownie, have ready ½ cup of water, simmering. Sift the powdered sugar into a mixing bowl. Melt the butter in a double boiler, turn off the heat, and add the chocolate. Stir until the chocolate and butter are both melted. Add the vanilla. Immediately whisk the chocolate mixture into the powdered sugar. With an electric mixer or a whisk, beat until blended. Slowly beat in boiling water until the mixture is creamy and shiny. When this occurs, do not add any more water.

Spread the frosting on the cooled brownies in a thin coat, only enough to cover, and set aside to firm. After 1 hour, return and cut the brownies to the desired size; I recommend cutting them into 2-inch squares.

❧ Chocolate Mousse

MAKES 3 CUPS—OR SIX ½-CUP SERVINGS
This mousse can be used as the base for a number of chocolate desserts. It has a wonderfully light texture.

6 ounces semisweet chocolate pieces
5 tablespoons unsalted butter
4 eggs, separated

1 tablespoon orange liqueur, such as Grand Marnier, Curaçao,
and so on (optional)
Whipped cream (for topping)

In the top of a double boiler, over very hot, not boiling water, melt the chocolate pieces with the butter, stirring as it melts. When melted, remove the entire double boiler from the heat and beat in the egg yolks, one at a time (leave the double boiler intact). Return the double boiler to the stove over a low flame and stir steadily for 5 minutes. Remove the double boiler from the heat and let the mixture sit in the double boiler for 5 more minutes. If using, add the liqueur. Separate the double boiler sections and set the chocolate/butter mixture aside.

In a large bowl, beat the egg whites until very stiff (by hand or with an electric beater). With a whisk, using an under/over motion, gently fold the chocolate mixture into the whites until no white streaks remain. Turn the bowl during this process. Pour the mousse into a 1-quart serving dish, or individual dessert dishes, and refrigerate to set, about 1 hour.

Serve with a dollop of whipped cream.

❧ Frozen Chocolate Mousse Crêpes with Crème Anglaise

This is my favorite dessert. It requires more work than most of the recipes in this book, but it makes a spectacular impression on guests. We did not serve this at the café, but Susan often made it for celebratory meals in our community. This is one dish that should be made at least a day ahead. The following recipe will make 14 crêpes. (Most people will want at least 2; I could han-dle 3.)

Crêpes

MAKES 14

⅔ cup all-purpose flour
⅓ cup sugar
2 eggs, well beaten
1½ tablespoons unsweetened cocoa powder
1 cup plus 2 tablespoons milk, at room temperature
¼ teaspoon salt
2 teaspoons vanilla extract
1 tablespoon melted butter

In a large bowl, whisk all the crêpe ingredients together until smooth. Cover and refrigerate at least 1 hour before making the crêpes.

Heat a crêpe pan or skillet over medium heat. Prepare the pan by spraying with oil or melting a touch of butter (you will not need to add butter or oil again). To make a crêpe, pour 2 tablespoons of batter into the pan, swirling the pan to spread the batter evenly. Within 2 minutes, loosen the sides of the crêpe with a rubber spatula. Flip the crêpe, using the spatula and your fingers, and cook for a few seconds on the other side, so that both sides are dry.

Transfer the hot crêpes to a tray or platter. Do not stack crêpes while hot. When cool, stack them.

Set the finished crêpes aside until you are ready to fill them with mousse. Refrigerate them if you will not be assembling the dish for a few hours.

Mousse Filling

MAKES 4 CUPS, ENOUGH FOR 14 CRÊPES

Prepare Chocolate Mousse (page 220), incorporating these changes: Omit the egg whites and double all other ingredients. Refrigerate until the mousse firms into a dense, creamy, pudding-like chocolate filling, about 1 hour.

Crème Anglaise (Vanilla Sauce)

3 cups whole milk
2 vanilla beans (If beans are not available, use 1 tablespoon vanilla extract, but this is not as tasty.)
6 tablespoons white sugar
6 egg yolks

Pour the milk into the top of a double boiler. Split the vanilla beans down the center and thoroughly scrape the insides into the milk. Add the pods to the milk with the sugar. Heat the mixture, stirring regularly, until it feels hot.

In a bowl, whisk the egg yolks lightly. Add 2 tablespoons of hot milk to the yolks and stir.

Remove the vanilla pods from the hot milk and set them aside. Gradually add the yolk mixture into the hot milk, stirring steadily, over medium heat. When the egg/milk mixture reaches 170 degrees (it takes about 8 minutes) it should begin to coat the spoon. Remove it from the heat as soon as it shows signs of thickening. Pour the mixture through a strainer into a clean, airtight container, put the vanilla pods back in, and chill.

To Assemble Crêpes

Place 2 rounded tablespoons of mousse filling on the bottom half of a crêpe. Spread it slightly, then roll up the crêpe, squeezing the filling to ¾ of an inch from each edge. Place the crêpe on a freezer-proof platter lined with waxed paper. Continue to fill all the crêpes, filling platter(s), putting wax paper between the layers to prevent sticking. Cover the platter with foil or plastic wrap and freeze at least 4 hours, preferably overnight.

Take the crêpes from the freezer 30 minutes before serving. Remove the vanilla pods from the crème anglaise and whisk one final time. Warm the sauce in a double boiler over low heat. Should the sauce begin to separate (the egg will appear to be cooking), pour the sauce through a strainer before serving. This will restore it to its creamy state. Gently separate the crêpes and place 2 on each plate. Ladle about 2 tablespoons of crème anglaise across the top of the crêpes, and serve. Garnish with mint leaves and a fresh or frozen red raspberry, if available. Put any extra sauce in little pitchers and serve with the crêpes.

❧ Susan's Old-Fashioned Moist Chocolate Cake

Susan feels that there are four factors for successful cake baking: using the highest-quality ingredients, especially the chocolate; having the ingredients at room temperature; proper and accurate measuring; and careful baking, making sure your oven is accurate and even (you can learn more about how your oven performs by buying an oven thermometer and periodically checking the temperature, especially for variations on each shelf and in the corners). You will see these concerns reflected in her recipe and instructions for this cake.

There has been so much emphasis in restaurants on tortes, cremes, and original "architectural" creations that cakes seem to have taken a back seat. These are cyclical patterns; some things will never go out of fashion. This is for those special times when only a cake will do. And what a cake!

1¾ cups cake flour
1 teaspoon baking powder
¼ teaspoon salt
½ teaspoon baking soda
½ cup Dutch-process cocoa powder (see Note; Hershey's
     European Style works well)
¼ pound sweet butter, at room temperature
1 teaspoon vanilla extract
1¾ cups white sugar
4 large eggs, at room temperature
1¼ cups buttermilk, at room temperature
Creamy Chocolate Frosting (see below)

Preheat the oven to 350 degrees (300 degrees if using a convection oven), making sure the oven rack is in the center of the oven. Grease two 9-inch cake pans with butter, shortening, or a spray oil such as Pam or Vegeline. Cut waxed or parchment paper circles to fit in the bottom of each pan. Place the circles in the pans. Grease the paper and then lightly dust each pan with flour (including the sides). Tap and shake out any excess flour. Set the pans aside.

In a mixing bowl, measure out 1¾ cups cake flour, unsifted. Sift it and remeasure. Keep exactly 1¾ cups and return the excess to the bag. Add to the flour the baking powder, salt, baking soda, and cocoa. Stir with a whisk or French whip until the ingredients are thoroughly mixed and the color is spread evenly. Then sift this twice to complete the blending (these steps are necessary to ensure a cake with no streaks); set aside.

At medium-high speed with an electric mixer, or with an electric hand mixer, cream the butter. Add the vanilla and sugar and beat for 1 minute. Add the eggs, one at a time, making sure each egg is incorporated before adding the next.

Reduce the mixer to the lowest speed to add the remaining ingredients. Mix in one third of the dry ingredients just until incorporated. Then add half of the buttermilk, adding slowly and scraping down the sides of the bowl with a rubber spatula; mix until just incorporated. Repeat, and finish with the final third of dry ingredients. Beat only until each addition is blended in, taking care not to overbeat.

Divide the batter evenly between the prepared cake pans. Spread the batter from the center to the edge of each pan so that the outer edge is slightly raised (this helps the cake bake more evenly). Place the pans on the center rack in the oven and bake 30 to 35 minutes, or until the edges begin to pull away from the side of the pan and the tops spring back in the center when lightly touched. Be careful not to overbake.

Remove the cakes from the oven and rest on cooling racks for 5 minutes to set. To remove from the pans, it will take two cooling racks for each cake. Cover the top of the cake with one rack and invert the pan. Remove the pan and the paper liner. Quickly invert again to the other rack, so that the cake is right side up. Let the layers sit until completely cool to the touch. Ice with Creamy Chocolate Frosting, using plenty of it between the layers.

N O T E : Dutch-process cocoa is alkylized and generally darker than regular cocoa, giving a smoother flavor to cakes. It also reacts differently to the baking soda and powder than regular cocoa.

Creamy Chocolate Frosting

MAKES 3 CUPS, ENOUGH TO FROST TWO 9-INCH LAYERS

3 tablespoons unsalted butter
6 ounces unsweetened baking chocolate (Ghirardelli or best available)
1 teaspoon vanilla extract
2 cups powdered sugar
1 cup heavy cream, warmed

In a double boiler (setting the inside pan over, not in, simmering water), slowly melt the butter and chocolate (the slower the better, to prevent the cocoa butter from separating out, which causes a milky film called "bloom"). As soon as the mixture begins to melt, remove the double boiler from the stove and allow it to finish melting. When melted, add the vanilla.

Put the melted chocolate in a mixing bowl, or in the bowl of an electric mixer. Add the powdered sugar slowly while you mix, scraping the sides regularly to incorporate everything. If you do not have an electric mixer, use an electric hand mixer or a wire whisk. Add the warm cream and beat thoroughly, until smooth and satiny.

To assemble the cake: Frost the first layer, then put the second layer on top and finish frosting the entire cake. Let the cake sit 30 minutes for the frosting to set.

❧ Chocolate-Covered Raspberries

MAKES 16 PIECES

This is a simple yet impressive dessert to serve company, and it is great fun to make with children. It was made for Brother Juniper's by two of our friends, Gene and Leslie Frank, of Forestville. Gene and Leslie are master potters who make ceremonial Jewish porcelain ceramics that are sold throughout the world under the name Ceramic Judaica. Gene and Leslie also grow raspberries and wild blackberries, so as a sideline that helped us quite a bit, they made chocolate-covered raspberries for the café.

12 ounces semisweet chocolate chips
1 tablespoon orange or raspberry liqueur (optional)
One ½-pint basket fresh raspberries, or blackberries, or
   boysenberries
16 petit-four papers (or muffin cup liners)

In a double boiler, melt the chocolate chips slowly. When the chocolate is smooth, add the liqueur, if using.

Place enough berries in each petit-four paper to half fill it. Spoon about 1 tablespoon melted chocolate over the berries, covering them. Place 1 berry on top of the melted chocolate. Chill for 1 hour, until the chocolate is hardened. Keep cool until ready to serve.

A Life Lesson with Grand

Marnier Soufflé

❧ During the second year of Brother Juniper's Café some friends of my parents came to San Francisco and invited Susan and me to join them for dinner. They chose a famous old restaurant, Ernie's, because they had once, many years before, had a memorable meal there. We had a wonderful time with them. The husband was in his eighties, his wife about eight to ten years younger. They were preparing for a trip to the Orient, a place of many fond memories for them as they had been in the import business and visited the Far East numerous times. They seemed to feel that this might be their last trip together, which turned out to be a true premonition when the husband died shortly after their return. On this night at Ernie's they taught us a life lesson.

The meal was excellent, a delicious blending of both classical and modern and quite a treat for two overworked cooks under a spiritual vow of poverty; but we were more entranced with our hosts. They told us stories of their life together, shared some of their wisdom of the business world, asked insightful questions about Brother Juniper's, and offered useful advice about growing a business. We heard the romantic story of their honeymoon and the first dessert they shared in France, a Grand Marnier soufflé. One of the reasons they chose Ernie's restaurant was because of the Grand Marnier soufflé, which they ordered for the four of us. They tried to have it at least once a year as it brought back all the good memories of their life together.

On our seventh anniversary Susan and I were, at long last, able to get away for a romantic weekend. We drove to Monterey, the home of John Steinbeck's Cannery Row, a world-famous aquarium featuring baby sea otters and a huge collection of jellyfish, a scenic view of the California coastline, and a restaurant called Fresh Cream known, among other things, for its Grand Marnier soufflé.

We could not actually afford to eat dinner at the restaurant, but we called them and ordered soufflé for two at 9:00 P.M. After a wonderful dinner at a less expensive place we walked to the other, along the edge of Monterey Bay, reminiscing about our first Grand Marnier soufflé at Ernie's. It had been five years and, frankly, I could not remember what the soufflé tasted like, only how the evening felt, the love between my parent's friends, and the spark of romance it kindled in us.

The people at the restaurant treated us royally, even pouring us some complimentary port as an anniversary gift. The soufflé was superb, the music was just right, everything was perfect. We were, for a few moments, at the center of the universe, and nothing else existed; no past hurts, no future fears, just the two of us and our Grand Marnier soufflé. It was another kind of magic.

❧ Grand Marnier Soufflé for Two

You will need two 1-cup (4-inch) ramekins (ovenproof soufflé cups) in which to bake these. To prepare the ramekins you need ½ teaspoon melted butter and 1 teaspoon granulated sugar.

Soufflé

2 large eggs, separated

1 tablespooon plus 1 teaspoon Grand Marnier or other orange
liqueur

Zest of 1 orange

6½ tablespoons granulated sugar

½ tablespoon powdered sugar

Grand Marnier Sauce

3 egg yolks

¼ cup white sugar

¼ cup Grand Marnier or other orange liqueur

½ cup heavy cream, whipped until thick

Preheat the oven to 450 degrees (do not make these in a convection oven), moving the rack to the bottom position. Butter the ramekins and sprinkle the insides with the teaspoon of sugar and set aside.

In a mixing bowl, combine the egg yolks, orange liqueur, zest, and half of the granulated sugar.

In another bowl, whip the egg whites until they form soft peaks, using either a wire whisk or electric or hand beaters. Slowly add the remaining granulated sugar and continue beating until the whites are stiff but not grainy.

Fold one-third of the egg whites into the yolks. When blended, gently fold in the remaining whites.

Fill the prepared ramekins to the top with the soufflé base, leveling it with a spatula. Wipe off the outside of each ramekin. Run your thumb around the inside edge of each ramekin, making a small indentation between the filling and the cup (this helps it rise more evenly).

Place the ramekins on the bottom shelf of the oven. Bake for 15 to 18 minutes, or until golden brown. The soufflés will rise approximately 1½ inches or more above the rim of the ramekin.

While the soufflés are baking, make Grand Marnier Sauce: In a heavy-bottomed stainless steel saucepan, mix the egg yolks and sugar until smooth. Do not use an aluminum pan for this. Over low heat, cook slowly, stirring constantly, until the mixture coats a wooden spoon. Remove the pan from the heat, stir in the liqueur, and fold in the whipped cream until blended. Serve warm in a small pitcher or creamer. If making in advance, refrigerate the sauce until needed. Warm it in a double boiler before serving.

When the soufflés are ready, sprinkle powdered sugar on the top of each. Then poke a hole in the top and pour Grand Marnier Sauce into the center. Serve immediately.

Epilogue:

When a Disc Bulges

*Grace takes us all to its bosom and proclaims general
amnesty.*
Babette's Feast

❧ It was on Christmas Day, 1988, that Brother Juniper's
broke our back. More accurately, it broke Susan's back. After
closing the café early on Christmas Eve, she spent hours wrapping gifts and buying groceries for a large family that the "Poor
People's Cup" had adopted. She then went Christmas caroling at
Victoria House, a home for developmentally disabled adults,
some of whom worked for us. Then there was a midnight mass
followed by a few hours of sleep. The pace was just too great.
While opening presents on Christmas morning two of her lower
back discs herniated. Fortunately, the orthopedic surgeon we
took her to advised against surgery. She began the laborious process of rehabilitation at the same time that we were scheduled to
begin our first expansion.

Thankfully, a few of members of our community, Br. Jacob
Friedman and Br. Allan and Sr. Geraldine Richardson, stepped in
to cover. Later Fr. Stephen Steineck and Br. Robert DeLucia also
joined with us.

I realized then that we had created something that was too big for us to carry. It was not the weight of the business, it was the weight of the vision; but we were past the point of no return and there was too much momentum to turn back. The primary objectives had been accomplished during the first two years: We were accepted by the general community, a form of ministry was being performed, our food was received with great enthusiasm, and our reputation was spreading beyond our hometown. Now we were faced with going on without Susan's daily presence and attention to details.

A major concern was that I needed to be at both the new bakery facility as well as the café. Fortunately, we had a good day crew to run the café. This allowed me to stay at the bakery from early morning until five in the afternoon and then, after a short dinner break, run the evening crew at the café. The bad news was that Susan was left alone most of the day with only our two wild kittens, Stashka and Minskey, to keep her company. By the time I got home it was usually about ten o'clock. I had just enough energy to discuss the day's events, and then crash.

We were living in a small cabin at the far end of our Forestville retreat center, deep in the woods and high on a hill, a mile from the entrance gate, with no telephone. After two months of this crazy juggling act we moved to a small apartment complex in Santa Rosa, where some other members of our community lived. This, at least, kept us in touch with civilization and put less stress on Susan's back while she healed.

Despite the setbacks, *"grace took us to its bosom"* and the bakery began to grow. Distributors approached us wanting to carry the bread. Soon we were in a number of good restaurants and markets. Production went from eighty loaves a day to two hundred and then to four hundred. We expanded twice, breaking through the walls into the facilities on either side of us and, ultimately, running out of room for further growth. Four years from when we began and two years from when we first moved into the new bakery facility, we were up to eight hundred loaves per day, graduating from small convection ovens to a five-shelf revolving oven. Our mixers were larger—everything was larger. It was like getting bigger and bigger toys.

Then we got an offer to move into an abandoned tortilla factory a few blocks from where we lived in Santa Rosa. There was three times as much space, which seemed ample, we naively thought. We made the move, installing a bigger oven, a bigger proof box, and bigger coolers. Within three years we were pressing against the seams of this building, trying to find room for simple things like desks, inventory, and cooling space for the bread.

Finally, seven years from when we first opened, Susan and I sold Brother Juniper's Bakery to another couple, Ron and Lorene Colvin. We had exhausted our resources as entrepreneurs. Susan's back still allowed only a part-time involvement and, with the foundation laid, we felt it time to see if the "baby" could walk without us. Ron and Lorene brought a fresh energy and had much more of a business background, yet a strong desire to continue the ministry aspect of the company. They enthusiastically jumped in and immediately sales increased by 20 percent. They are, as I write, working around the clock to fulfill the vision we all share for Brother Juniper's future. This includes the expansion into some of the products developed in the café, such as sauces (Holy Smoke is already on the shelves), salad dressings, sodas, and mixes for bread machines.

We survived the broken back, and out of the struggle something quite unique emerged. When looking back I experience a wide range of emotions. Many people have said, "You must be proud of what you created." Like many small business owners, we are proud of our accomplishments but they did not come easily or without a price. The phrase, "No pain, no gain," is apt.

Here is what we really gained: When people come together to share a meal a bond is formed. As the anthropologist Jack Goody writes, "Those who eat and drink together are by this very act tied to one another by a bond of friendship and mutual obligation."* If the word *religion* simply means, as its roots indicate, *to be connected,* then our religious community extended to the people we fed through Brother Juniper's Café. These were, for three intense years, the folks with whom we ate and drank, forming undeniable bonds of "friendship and mutual obligation." It was our extended community and, as such, we shared through the magic of food a type of communion. Our culinary skills grew in proportion to our sacramental experience.

Success in feeding people can only be measured, ultimately, by the lives that are touched and the quality of that touch. In the case of Brother Juniper's Café that quality is called *agape.* It means love of the highest order, spiritual love. Touching lives, connecting, is the memory of Brother Juniper's Café that sustains us. It is the magic I will always remember.

*Jack Goody, *Cooking, Cuisine, and Class* (Cambridge University Press, 1982), p. 12.

Index